"There are few people in the world with Lisa Aschmann's grasp on the songwriting process and the catalogue to prove it. The insights she shares in this book will nurture and inspire songwriters at all levels—from seasoned pros to those new to the craft. It is chock full of block-busting tools and ideas that will keep any artist firmly on their creative path."

—Lowry Olafson, songwriter

"Lisa has the gift of deep appreciation. She finds the preciousness—the exquisite value—of bees, and pears, and almond blossoms and then, wonder of wonders, she pulls words out of heaven to help the rest of us see and hear along with her. More than a generator of ideas, she's a discoverer of ideas hanging ripe on hidden trees, waiting to be plucked and tasted. She's also a sweetheart. I can't think of a better guide to the wonderful mind-space of song."

—John Tirro, songwriter

"Lisa is an enthusiastic and inspiring teacher, nurturer, and friend to hundreds of aspiring as well as accomplished songwriters. I am thankful as an aspiring songwriter that she has provided out-of-class materials through her books that have made me a better songwriter, and even a better person. On that last part, you'll know what I mean as you read her book."

—David Alexander, Ph.D., business professor and songwriter

"I've been a fan of Lisa Aschmann's book, 500 Songwriting Ideas: for Brave and Passionate People, since it was first released, recommending it in my own book. Now she's got 1000 ideas. If you know what you want to write about and you're not sure how to approach it, this is a great kick-start. If you don't know what you want to say, it can give you that first healthy pull that starts that creative siphon flowing. A wealth of fun assignments, exercises, tools, and inspiration. Unique!"

—John Braheny, author of The Craft and Business of Songwriting

"Lisa is one of my very favorite co-writers. Her brilliant mind leads us to strange and wonderful places. I have used many of her 1000 Songwriting Ideas in my songwriting classes."

—Karen Taylor-Good, songwriter

"Aside from her ability to craft some of the most intelligent, witty and warm lyrics and storylines I've ever heard, Lisa has a musician's integrity for creating beautiful melodies and chord structures. The fact that she does not play an instrument keeps her out of the rut of musical mediocrity that many songwriters fall into. Lisa's songs are "ear candy.""

—Don Jones, songwriter and national finger-style guitar champion

"I have been a friend, fan, and co-conspirator with Lisa Aschmann for more than a dozen years, and I can state, unequivocally, Lisa's mind has no boundaries and her ability is only shackled by the hours of the day. She typifies my own mantra, "knowledge is power." This body of work is an invaluable piece of creative machinery with which the blossoming writer and the already successful and creative can discover something new at the turn of any page. I highly recommend it!"

—Wayne Carson, songwriter

"There is an un-self-consciousness about a truly gifted person. A person who is truly gifted sails just ahead of their own creativity. If you read this book, you will step into that world and find it catching."

—Louisa Branscomb, songwriter

"A book to really rattle that "creative cage" we writers get trapped in from time to time. Wonderfully inspiring, joyously instructional… sometimes it's great just doing the ridiculous."

—Joni Bishop, songwriter

"There is so much more to this book than ideas for songs. This book, the encouragement it gives, and the drive to write are all anyone needs to know the joy of writing songs. A song doesn't need to be a "hit" to be great; it only needs to be started and sung by those who love it."

—Janet Peterson, songwriter and site coordinator
of Puget Sound Guitar Workshop

by Lisa Aschmann

HAL•LEONARD®

Hal Leonard Books
An Imprint of Hal Leonard Corporation
New York

Published in 2008 by Hal Leonard Books
An Imprint of Hal Leonard Corporation
19 West 21st Street, New York, NY 10010

Printed in USA

Book and cover design by Stephen Ramirez
Photos courtesy of Dark Horse Recording, Franklin, TN

Library of Congress Cataloging-in-Publication Data is available upon request.

ISBN 978-1-4234-5440-3

www.halleonard.com

Acknowledgments

I'd like to thank (so I'm going to) the staff and students of the Puget Sound Guitar Workshop (PSGW), especially John Miller, Becky and John Knowles, Ray Bierl, Bob Brozman, Joe Vinikow, Chris Grampp, Peter Langston, Kim Scanlon, Tom Rawson, Marcia Taylor, Daniel Steinberg, and Janet Peterson, for putting bees in my bonnet and helping me get started; Larry Joba for typing this; and other teaching friends and writers for their creativity, such as Elaine Farris Hughes, Buddy Kaye, Dick Goodwin, Rick Beresford, K. A. Parker, Cat Cohen, Janis Stevenson, Doug Hall, and Steve Gillette. This started out as class material for the Puget Sound Guitar Workshop and sort of mushroomed. It's a good climate for mushrooms up there on the Olympic Peninsula . . .

I don't even play an instrument, and I've written 2,000 songs. My friends are the reasons why. Bill Piburn, Jamey Whiting, Jim Lewin, John Haley-Walker, Catesby Jones, Joel Evans, David Toby, Michael Johnson, Pat Bergeson, Rick Dougherty, Don Carlisle, Scott Musick, Ron Troutman, John Smith, Kerry Marx, Fred Koller, Frank Baldwin, David West, Joel Plimmer, Jerry Styner, John Tirro, Richard Follett, Michael Lounibos, Jack Fischer, Rolf Wyer, Jeff Lewis, David Vasquez, Gary Pickus, Larry Batiste, Jack Pearson, Lindy Hearne, Ron Kristy, Bob Patin, Bobby Pinson, Dorian Michaels, David Alexander, Michael Behymer, Tom Kimmel, Michael Lille, Mike Williams, Paul Alan Smith, Mark Burchfield, Jim Burrill, Henry Hipkens, Kent Blazy, Woody Mann, John Mock, Roger Day, David Bartky, Steve Parrish, Tim Johnson, Tim Mathews, Dan Marcus, Jimmy Jackson, Rick Ryan, Barry Fasman, Wayne Carson, Mark Simos, Robert Berry, Tom Doty, Dan E. Strymer, Howard Schwartz, Tom Fox, Michael Harmon, Kevin Carr, Tom Paxton, Roger Linn, Bob Reid, Ray Frank, Sam Weedman, Jim Nunnally, Don Jones, Lowry Olafsen, Danny Timms—and *so* on, the list goes on and on—Joni Bishop, Nancy Conescu, Joyce Woodson, Betsy Jackson, Marilyn Hencken, Sandy

ACKNOWLEDGMENTS

Sherman, Lena Lucas, Jane Murray, Kate Wallace, Francis Glascoe, Janice Carper, Carol McComb, Bethany Dick, Becky Buller, Irene Kelley, Helen White, Karen Taylor Good, Sally Barris, Carol Hashe, Ellen Daros, jael, Ellen Britton, Lynn Langham, Lynne Robin Green, Barbara Mendelsohn, Karee Wardrop, Cee Jay McDuffy, Piper Heisig, Noel Cash, Joyce Rouse, Sonny Ochs, Patti and Michael Silversher—oh, it could go on a long time, this list! These people have co-written and arranged and backed me up and encouraged me like nobody's business and respected me and my musical ideas, too. It takes a genuinely great spirit to let somebody learn on your time. Thanks, you guys!

Larry Joba, my hero, worked like a navvy on this, typing, getting permission to use quotes, and checking references. Thank you, Larry! Special thanks are due my daughter Amelia for the initial edition's cover art and to all my children for staying off the computer while all this was going on. And thanks to Lisa Duran and the staff of MixBooks for staying on through the same. Thanks to Mike Lawson and Barbara Sharp Milbourn, my publisher and editor respectively, who not only championed this book but typed and edited it and supplied me with DVD's, tea, and sympathy for my broken leg.

As this is a book on songwriting, I've tried to give credit to the writer of the songs I mention. I thank—we all thank—them for their wonderful songs. On the other hand, I apologize if I have omitted or made mistakes in attribution. This is just part of my mental library, and some of the shelves are pretty empty. Sorry! It's a tribute to these songs that the very mention of a title or a line from them is recognizable, and as such, there really is no losing sight of their origins. That certainly wasn't intended.

My thank-yous wouldn't be complete without mentioning two of my writers in memoriam, Georgia Yates and Molly Finkle, two fine lyricists in the Bay Area. As Georgia used to ask when I walked into the room, "What's *on*? Your *mind*?

Contents

Introduction to the First 500 Songwriting Ideas

One of the most pernicious words in the English language, in my view, is "genius." Another one is "talent." These words divide people and keep them from accessing what is native to them: their own creativity. Genius mystifies what is readily available. Creativity is an immediately accessible, widely distributed birthright. People are smart, but they're afraid to look dumb. And they think that others, unlike themselves, have something special. They think that they require something special, some prerequisite skill/talent/genius before they can give themselves permission to let go and let their ideas flow freely. They let their editor/critic/censor kick in before they just do it: problem solve and generate new songs. It doesn't work like that. Be fearless. Be thought inept, crazy, foolish, and a terrible writer or musician. Let them laugh but write anyway. My motto is: Dare to be stupid.

It's not that I believe in or endorse stupidity. It's the daring that counts. Fear is the gatekeeper to the floodgates of inspiration. Also, "beginner mind," an attitude of ignorance, is useful. The best inoculation from learning something is knowing it already. So, dare to begin and begin again. There are two main impediments to being creative. One is being overly critical. The other is being overly awed. (Being overly odd may help.) But if we're all down here making monkeys of ourselves and ordinary mortals write songs, then you, too, can dare to be stupid.

Anybody can write songs. Especially, brave and passionate people can write songs. People like us risk looking stupid in order to create something new. Our love of music is stronger than our fear of rejection.

INTRODUCTION

These are creativity exercises. Some suggestions have to do with music, others have to do with language, still others have to do with loosening up, and some have to do with finding inspiration in what others have done before you. Keeping an open mind is good for songwriting, even if that means sometimes restricting yourself to some tried and true forms. As Maya Angelou says, "I know why the caged bird sings." So do I; it's because of the cage, not in spite of it. Creativity is set free within the confines of form and game playing. Lighten up. These are arbitrary, silly exercises.

Face it; you're going to have to write some duds to get to the gems. I figure I'm well into the first phase of this, so any day now I might write a keeper. Go, thou, and do likewise.

500 Songwriting Ideas

Dare to be stupid. A thing worth doing is worth doing anyway.

— 1 —

Turn off the sound on the TV and write conversations for the soap operas.

— 2 —

Eavesdrop at a café.

— 3 —

Study advertisements. How is something bigger, newer, more compact, faster?

How is pleasure promised? How is "better" shown?

Advertising appeals to our core needs. People may own a certain car because it makes them feel freer or richer or sexier than people who don't. Advertisers push universal buttons that address those needs. So do hit songs. Here are some needs people could use your reassurance on: sex, validation, safety, excitement, security, individuality, intelligence, status, to be famous, important, noticed, to be thought attractive, powerful, top dog, popular, ahead of the trends, eco-friendly.

These are some needs you could address that are dear to your listeners. By using advertising, product-design, and song you might even meet some of these needs.

— 4 —

Make up life stories of people in stores, airports, or bus terminals.

— 5 —

Plan a series of sermons or lessons about life.

Finish these phrases:

_____when all fails.

The first/last thing my mom/dad told me was _____.

I was born to _____.

You can always count on _____ to _____.

I wouldn't trade a million bucks for _____.

— 6 —

Imagine that body parts or household objects have feelings.
What would this door, mirror, table, picture, heart, wall
say if it could talk?

— 7 —

Imitate the rhythms of nursery rhymes, e.g., "Jack Sprat could eat no fat . . ."

"Ride a cock horse to Banbury Cross . . ."

"Little Miss Muffet sat on a tuffet . . ."

— 8 —

Translate poetry from a language you don't know.

— 9 —

Fracture some fairy tales. Retell a movie plot.

— 10 —

Explain earthlings to aliens; what are our customs for?

— 11 —

What would you like to tell your hero/favorite teacher/child? Write an important letter to someone you know.

— 12 —

Define these terms: home, a life worth living, the perfect day, what I want most, the greatest gift, my dream lover.

— 13 —

Use counterfactuals. If _____ weren't true, then I'd be a monkey's uncle, e.g., "Till the Rivers All Run Dry" (Don Williams and Wayland Holyfield), "If Ever I Would Leave You" (Alan Jay Lerner and Frederick Loewe), ("I've got some") "Ocean Front Property" ("in Arizona . . .") (Garland Cochran, Royce Porter, and Dean Dillon).

— 14 —

Create switcheroos, e.g., "Not only are things seldom what they seem, but they never were" (Marshall Barer). Look for true paradoxes, opposites, contrasts, e.g., "Up is Down" (Marshall Barer), "Full Moon and Empty Arms" (Buddy Kaye and Ted Mossman), "Come Rain or Come Shine" (Johnny Mercer and Harold Arlen), "The Night We Called It a Day" (Thomas Adair and Matt Dennis), "The Last Thing I Needed the First Thing This Morning . . ." (Gary P. Nunn and Sam Farar).

— 15 —

Make lists of synonyms, metaphors, and similes and use them to create titles or first lines. A good exercise to do along these lines is to finish the phrase "as quiet as a _____," and don't say "mouse";

"as hard as a _____," and don't say "rock";

"as light as a _____," and don't say "feather," etc.

— 16 —

List things that go together, e.g., socks and shoes, salt and pepper, "Leather and Lace" (Graeme Pleeth), "We Were Meant to Be Together" (Jeffrey Taylor), "Scotch and Soda" (Dave Guard).

— 17 —

Count things, e.g., "Eighteen Wheels and a Dozen Roses" (Paul Nelson and Gene Nelson), "The Twelve Days of Christmas," "If the Devil Danced" ("in empty pockets, he'd have a ball in mine, with a 9-foot grand, a 10-piece band, and a 12-foot chorus line.") (Kim Williams and Ken Spooner). There are eighty-eight keys on a piano, four quarts in a gallon, two-lane highways, a first and last what?

— 18 —

List the best of things, e.g., Cole Porter's "You're the Top," "Cadillac Style" (Mark Petersen), "You Take the Cake" (Joseph Garland), Godiva chocolates.

— 19 —

Use onomatopoeia, sounds that "say themselves": RRRRRING, BEEEEP, BLAM! For instance, you could imitate a train whistle as Tom Kimmel does in his song "Blue Train," which he wrote with Jennifer Kimball. Repetition of certain syllables can make flute-like, bell-like, or train-like sounds, e.g., "piccolo meeny" sounds like a piccolo when repeated fast and high. "Chicken fricassee" or "a ticket in a pocket" when repeated can sound like train wheels. Some three-part rounds or spoken pieces are designed with that effect in mind, e.g., "Soup," "One Bottle of Pop," etc.

— 20 —

What does nature sound like? For instance, "The wind in the willows, sighing like a solitary soul alone . . ."

— 21 —

Write about a favorite city, state, place. Use qualities of the place to describe a person or a feeling, e.g., Hoagy Carmichael and Stuart Gorrell's "Georgia on My Mind."

— 22 —

Walk. Walk in different rhythms. Two-step, waltz, tap your feet, slide, run, spin, clap your hands, wave your arms, wag your head. Get funky and see what song suggests itself to you.

— 23 —

Write twenty ways to say "I Love You" without using the word "love" and twenty ways to say "good-bye" without saying "good-bye."

— 24 —

Make exceptions without using the word "but."

— 25 —

Motivate somebody to rebel against something.

— 26 —

What's the hardest thing you ever did? The easiest? What's your proudest moment? Your saddest moment? Go inward.

— 27 —

Pick somebody you admire and write about them.

— 28 —

Put music to different art forms. What would a Paul Klee sing like? A Vermeer? What is Rodin's *The Thinker* pondering?

— 29 —

Try intervals you've never tried before, even weird ones, like $1 \rightarrow 9$ as in "Walk Against the Wind" (Lisa Aschmann and David Bartky); or start with melodic tension that needs to be resolved, like Leonard Bernstein's "Maria" $1 \rightarrow {}^\flat 5 \rightarrow 5$.

— 30 —

Stick to a traditional genre. Try a traditional twelve-bar blues, dominant sevenths (four bars each of $1^{\flat 7}$, $4^{\flat 7}$, $5^{\flat 7}/1^{\flat 7}$, $4^{\flat 7}/1^{\flat 7}$).

Rules for writing the blues:

You can't begin a blues with the line, "I've got a good woman" unless the second line is, "with the baddest dog in town." Also, your name has to have a modifier (Blind, Old, Howlin'). It can't be Samantha, Brittany, or Cheyenne, and no matter how many men they shot in Memphis or Detroit, it can't be in Des Moines or Hackensack.

— 31 —

Write a canon or a round.

— 32 —

Illustrate a musical theory idea in a song.

"Circle of Fifths" (Raun McKinnon) or "One Note Samba" (Antonio Carlos Jobim)

— 33 —

Write a song for an occasion. Birthdays and christenings are good, as are weddings, farewells, and holidays. Or make up a holiday, call it by your own name, and say what you do to celebrate it. Alan O'Day and I wrote "It's Do Something Stupid Day." The Sherman Brothers wrote "Have a Very Merry Un-birthday."

— 34 —

Imitate a group's style. Write a newly discovered Beatles tune or an Andrews Sisters or Beach Boys song. Parody not only their lyrical style, but their harmony styles, e.g., "We Are Not Crosby, Stills, Nash, and Young" by RST.

— 35 —

Pick a rhythmic nonsense word or phrase and make it a centerpiece, e.g., "Diddy Wah Diddy" (Leon Redbone), "Da Doo Ron Ron" (Jeff Barry, Ellie Greenwich, and Phil Spector), fol de rol de rincum caddie, etc.

— 36 —

Make a list of your favorite words or the prettiest sounds you know and see if you can work them into a song somehow. Do that with your favorite chord progressions.

— 37 —

Remember what bugs you about certain people? Tell them off.

— 38 —

Have a dialogue with a kid. Sample topics: Why is the sky blue? Why did he/she/it have to die? What is the color of love? Where do you go when you go to sleep?

— 39 —

Tell a tall tale, e.g., "Darby Ram." Make it a whopper but try to make it plausible. For instance: That winter, we were so hungry we ate our words. That summer, it was so hot corn popped in the field.

— 40 —

You've met a genie. What are your three wishes?

— 41 —

You've met the Dalai Lama. What did he say? (I know what *you* say; you say, "Hello, Dolly!" [Jerry Herman].)

— 42 —

You've met your favorite actor or author. What do you do together?

— 43 —

Write in one of the modes you don't usually hear—like Aeolian (minor), Dorian (Celtic)—or use a harmonic minor key (e.g., Aeolian) but sharp the 7th or make the leading tone an augmented 2nd. In other words, alter a mode with accidentals to create special scales to give your music that flamenco or gypsy effect.

— 44 —

Adopt the point of view and voice of the opposite sex, and write from that perspective.

— 45 —

Think about why you believe or don't believe in God. Tell the story of how you came to believe or not believe.

— 46 —

Sing a song for your enemy. Who or what do you hate the most? Write about getting rid of it. Write about your own freedom.

— 47 —

Spell out the reasons why you stopped doing something you used to do.

— 48 —

Pick a pet or totem animal to honor.

— 49 —

Take us on a journey.

— 50 —

Write about a season of the year or a certain month.

— 51 —

What are your waking rituals and thoughts, your first, your last? Any prayers? Did you know you could *sing* grace before a meal?

— 52 —

Take a mental photograph. Pretend you're a movie camera. Pick a scene that has a process going on in it already, like a rodeo or a Coca-Cola bottling plant work day, where you could shoot from one angle indefinitely. Then play with camera conventions—freeze-frame, zoom lens, close-up, fisheye, fast forward, time lapse, flashback—and edit the scene. What if you could film something important in your life? What's different about TV versus reality? Headline the events you see. Parody journalistic style.

— 53 —

Write about inner versus outer experiences (what you say versus what you don't say in any given social scene), for example, "The Waltz," a short story by Dorothy Parker.

— 54 —

Try writing a story or a musical piece backward.

— 55 —

Write a musical palindrome.

— 56 —

Write your phone number, the Fibonacci series, Avogadro's number, pi, e, Planck's constant, license plates, street addresses, letters as numbers (1-26). In other words, randomize a sequence of notes or chords. One = 8 and 9 = 2 and 0 could be a rest but the rest of the number sequence could be scale degrees.

— 57 —

Make up a word and write about what it means. Start a gibberish conversation.

— 58 —

Mentally visit a carnival, museum, mental hospital, or zoo and tell about the exhibits, the experience, the crowd. Then, write about the widest, most open spaces you can think of, like the prairies, Alpha Centauri, etc.

— 59 —

Play with irony and sincerity. Write a heartfelt song and a really sarcastic one.

— 60 —

Write music over "Heart and Soul" (1 6 4 5 chords). This song by Hoagy Carmichael and Frank Loesser may be a great one, but it isn't the only great one, now is it?

— 61 —

If you weren't you, who would you be? Write about that person.

— 62 —

If there were a moon colony or a Martian colony, what would its national anthem sound like?

— 63 —

Write songs for stereotypical characters, like the hunk, the sex kitten, the old maid, the hustler, the innocent, the criminal, the cheater, the bartender, the night clerk, the taxi driver, the big spender (or use several in one song).

— 64 —

Imagine being sunlight or water.

— 65 —

Whatever happened to your first love? Tell the story or make up a story about what happened years later.

— 66 —

Think about the ground. How does it look in your hand? Underfoot? In an earthquake? An excavation? A garden? A farm? A rocky mountain top? Remember the last time you were really in touch with the earth. How did it feel? How about asphalt? Concrete? Write a song for one of these landscapes: the Alps, the Grand Canyon, the Everglades.

— 67 —

Write a song that you would have to whisper.

— 68 —

Write a song with the words *heart, night* or *if* in the title. These are the three most-often used words in hit song titles.

— 69 —

Write a heartfelt, emotional song without using the words *love, heart,* or *feel.*

— 70 —

Write a kid's song to teach counting or the alphabet.

— 71 —

Write a funny song; see if you can make the listener laugh.

— 72 —

Talk about aging from the point of view of regret (lost youth, etc.), rebellion, pity, or admiration, e.g., "Nick of Time" by Bonnie Raitt.

— 73 —

Write a song from a book or movie title.

— 74 —

Write a song titled a man or woman's name and really make them come alive as a character study. "Bad, Bad Leroy Brown" (Jim Croce)

— 75 —

Where would I be without you? Finish:

If it weren't for _____, I'd be _____.

— 76 —

Where are you most at peace?

— 77 —

Systematically take all of the intellect out of your song idea. As I heard a producer complain to a singer recently when he wanted him to re-sing a line: "Hey, I hear you *thinking* in there!" What he meant was get out of your head and into your heart. Scan what you're doing for intellectual versus emotional impact.
What's left after you *quit* thinking?

— 78 —

Pick objects that aggravate you and put them in the center of your song.

— 79 —

Try writing five kinds of love songs with you and your real or ideal lover in mind. (The most common type is #4.)

1. Write about the lover in the first person. "He's So Shy" (Tom Snow and Cynthia Weil)

2. Write about the lover in the second person. "Tell Laura I Love Her" (Jeff Barry and Ben Raleigh)

3. Write about the lover in the third person. "She's in Love With the Boy" (Jon Ims)

4. Write to the lover from the first person. Billy Joel's ("I love you") "Just the Way You Are"

5. Write about the relationship in first person plural. "We Belong" (Eric Lowen and Dan Navarro) and "Look at Us" (Vince Gill)

— 80 —

Here are some adjectives about love:

Immature/mature
Celestial

Divine
Passionate
Brotherly
Obsessive
Ravenous
Rapturous
Magnificent
Endless
Tender
Fiery
Star-crossed
Illicit
Devoted
Suffocating
Honest
Embracing
Delirious
Powerful
Innocent
Wild

What others can you think of?

— 81 —

Is it stale or is it style? Ask your friends to point out when your music "all sounds the same," then look for fresh material. Or, see if you can develop a really exact style for yourself by staying with similar topics, chord progressions, line lengths, grooves, etc.

— 82 —

Flip Breskin collects songs she calls "songs of compassion." Yes! Write one of these. What do your feet tell you after you've walked a mile in somebody else's moccasins?

— 83 —

Finish these phrases:

The only thing I care about is _____.

All I ever wanted was _____.

_____ is all I need.

_____ is all I've got left.

_____ is what I'm living for.

_____ means everything to me.

I've waited a lifetime for _____.

_____ is the most important thing in the world to me.

I'll be _____ as long as I have _____.

— 84 —

The bad news *is* the good news. Find some examples of this, e.g., you meet your prospective boss on the stuck elevator, Uncle Harry died and left you a million bucks. My friend, Max Cain, winning the lottery after his wife left him wrote, "You Got Off One Stop Early, Shirley."

— 85 —

Write a song about a job or an occupation, for example, "Drill Ye Tarriers, Drill."

— 86 —

Write about your heritage, your roots, the land(s) of your forefathers and foremothers.

— 87 —

Here's a romantic triangle plot: Boy meets girl, girl falls in love with boy's best friend. Write about sexual jealousy, betrayal, friendship, choices.

— 88 —

Write a series of negative injunctions:

Don't _____.
I'm not _____.

Note, though, that when you do this, you introduce the idea you're trying to negate. "Don't think of a camel" is a great way to get somebody to visualize a camel. And what about "I'm Not in Love" (David Byrne) or ("I ain't") "Missing You" (John Waite, Mark Leonard, and Charles Sandford)? Who believes them?

— 89 —

Write a song based on an old saying, platitude, homily, or aphorism, e.g., his bark was worse than his bite. There are more fish in the sea. An ounce of prevention is worth a pound of cure.

— 90 —

Set a recipe to music.

— 91 —

Write a cowboy song. 1 5 6 1, 1 5 6 1 . . .

— 92 —

Write a kid's song to teach some subject matter, like the history of your state or the names of trees.

— 93 —

Write about an invention or an inventor or an explorer.

— 94 —

Play with line lengths that are very wordy, as in "Auctioneer" by LeRoy Van Dike and Buddy Black, or sparse, as in "Soul Deep" by Wayne Carson. Try to write one-word, two-word, three-word, and four-word phrases with lots of space around the words. Restrict yourself to only four-syllable lines, as in Hank Williams' "Your Cheatin' Heart."

— 95 —

Write a song haiku or set an existing haiku to music. For instance, "Moonlight in Vermont" by John Blackburn and Karl Suessdorf is a haiku.

— 96 —

Think of the most nasal song you can, and write in that voice.

— 97 —

Think of the most throaty or breathless song you can, and write in that voice.

— 98 —

Play with the confusion of sexuality and religion (the way some of Madonna's songs do). Write something irreverent or as reverent as you can make it, using either sex or religion as the main topic. Like Rumi's poetry, romanticize the spiritual or spiritualize the romantic. It's all in how you refer to "The Beloved," and how you allegorize surrender.

— 99 —

Pick up an instrument you don't normally play and noodle a bit.

— 100 —

Make some sounds associated with repetitive gestures—like sewing, turning a waterwheel, hammering, chopping wood—and choreograph them.

— 101 —

Write about a vehicle (boat, car, plane, train, escalator).
Good examples are "If I had a Boat" and "Which Way Does That
Old Pony Run?" both by Lyle Lovett.

— 102 —

Write a swing tune called "Mood Swing" (Lou Barlow and John Davis)
or "The Swing Set" (Richard Bowles) or another pun that refers to a
musical style or instrument in the title. For example, "When I Was
Green, I didn't Have the Blues" (Lisa Aschmann and Fred Koller) or
"Sax Appeal" (Kim Waters). Write a song for a particular instrument
that illustrates its range and timbre.

— 103 —

Write a mystery or ghost story, e.g., "Long Black Veil"
by Danny Dill and Marijohn Wilkin.

— 104 —

Scatter five arbitrary nouns on a piece of paper down the page and then write in the spaces around them to fill in the meaning (like you do with Mad Libs).

— 105 —

Reverse syntax or the parts of speech. Make verbs act as nouns and nouns act as verbs or make adjectives nouns. For example, "Home" by Karla Bonoff.

"Home sings me of sweet things . . .
My life there has its own wings
Fly me over the mountain
Though I'm standing still . . ."

— 106 —

Use gerunds (present passive voice verbs), e.g., "Running With the Night" (Lionel Richie and Cynthia Weil) or "Flying Down to Rio" (Gus Kahn, Edward Eliscu, and Vincent Youmans).

— 107 —

Pick a meter and stick two or four bars of another meter in a section of the song, e.g., "Have a Heart" by Bonnie Hayes. Go out of step and insert extra notes or phrases in some places, deliberately crowding a line.

— 108 —

Use counter-rhythms or polyrhythms and write over them using a call-and-response form.

— 109 —

Establish a bass run that repeats and adds a counter-rhythm, e.g., "Lady Madonna" and "Blackbird" (Lennon and McCartney), "Liza (All the Clouds'll Roll)" (George Gershwin, Ira Gershwin, and Gus Kahn), "Fields of Gold" (Sting). Try walking a bass line that strays from the notes of the chord. In the key of C, the bass could go: $C \rightarrow A^\flat \rightarrow A \rightarrow G \rightarrow F$, for instance.

— 110 —

Write a song using an unusual rhythm, such as 3/2 or 5/8 time.

— 111 —

Make a song *about* rhythms, e.g., "I Like to Play in 7/8 Time" (Lisa Aschmann and Jamey Whiting).

— 112 —

Write a rap song.

— 113 —

Write a song using a Bo Diddley rhythmic motif, a Buddy Holly motif,
a Babyface motif (e.g., cop a groove).

— 114 —

Write a song about dancing. "I Could Have Danced All Night"
(Lerner and Loewe) or "You Make Me Feeling Like Dancing"
(Leo Sayer and Vincent Poncia)

— 115 —

Write a jump rope-skipping song. Examples: "In came the doctor, in
came the nurse, in came the lady with the alligator purse . . ."; "Not last
night but the night before, twenty-four robbers came knockin' at my
door . . ."; "Salt, pepper, vinegar, and wine . . ."

— 116 —

Switch a "straight" groove to "swing" or vice versa. Emphasize eighth
notes and/or triplets in a rhythm. Use straight 8's rock, a 12/8 ballad,
or a 4/4 swing feel. Use syncopation, e.g., rock ballad, swing feel. Louis
Jordan was a master at this type of changeover from straight to swing
and so was that other Louis, Louis Armstrong.

— 117 —

Think of as many sensual details as you can and cluster them around a particular sense, such as smell or touch.

— 118 —

Write a song that doesn't rhyme anywhere.

— 119 —

Write a song that rhymes in groups of three and then has one unrhymed word.

— 120 —

Meditate awhile. Write something that might get you in the mood to do this.

— 121 —

Copy somebody else's song form exactly, using their melody (write a parody), and then change the melody.

— 122 —

Here's a list of potential writing topics from Elaine Farris Hughes' book, *Writing from the Inner Self*:

Sensuous pleasures
Future daydreams
Things I'm keeping from myself
Good things about my life
Ways I'm unkind to myself
Unusual experiences I have had
The masks I wear
Old yearnings
New ambitions
All the things that are okay about me
All the things I want
People I miss
Childhood delights
Some gratitudes
Why I'll never be (or *will* be) a writer
Feelings that cause me the most trouble
Objects I have loved
My favorite room
What I think about men (or women)
My favorite songs or artists (this ought to stoke you like nothing else will;
listen to some great songs!)

— 123 —

Write a song about being fat (or thin), about dieting or eating,
e.g., "Rolly Poley" ("daddy's little fatty") by Fred Rose
or "Big Boned Gal" by k.d. lang.

— 124 —

What is it about you that is indestructible?

— 125 —

Use as many five-syllable adverbs as you can in a lyric, e.g., "I'm speaking to you confidentially . . ."

— 126 —

Write a song using only one-syllable words.

— 127 —

Two blind people going at it with hammer and scissors. Write about violence from an amused perspective. Shel Silverstein has some outrageous ones: "The Winner" and "Three Legged Man" come to mind.

Or, write about violence from a serious perspective. There are some great anti-war songs out there, but there can't be too many.

— 128 —

Think of things you do in fourth grade that stigmatize you for life.

— 129 —

Here we go again. Reflect on repetition, things that have happened over and over in history or in your personal relationships.

— 130 —

Write a song with only two chords, like "Tulsa Time" (Danny Flowers: 1, 5), "Achy Breaky Heart" (Don von Tress: 1, 5), "Just My Imagination Running Away With Me" (Barrett Strong and Norman Whitfield: 1, 5). How about using a two-chord form other than 1, 5? Try one with only three chords.

— 131 —

Write the bass line first.

— 132 —

Write the drum part first.

— 133 —

Write a song to heal a relationship.

— 134 —

Think of something about love you could exaggerate, e.g., "Forever," "Until the stars go out," "Your love can move mountains."

— 135 —

Write a graduation theme, a year's-end party song, a
let's-go-to-the-beach song.

— 136 —

Write a lullaby.

— 137 —

Jorge Luis Borges in his book, *On Writing*, quotes Oscar Wilde:
"Were it not for the sonnet or other set forms of verse, we would all
be at the mercy of genius." Well, I told you what I thought of genius!
By the way, W. B. Yeats, Kipling, and Robert Service are particularly
fertile fields of poetry for songwriters. They're some great poets who've
motivated excellent melodies. Set a sonnet or other tightly fixed form
of poetry to music. Personally, I have had songs inspired by the writings of Edwin Arlington Robinson, Mary Oliver, Robert Frost, Rumi,
St. John of the Cross, Sara Teasdale, and May Sarton. Try a strict-form
poem, a free-form poem. Set a poem to music.

— 138 —

Write a song that has a minor 7th in it, like ("there's a place for us")
"Somewhere" (Stephen Sondheim and Leonard Bernstein).

— 139 —

Write a song that has a major 7th in it, e.g., the second line of Henry Mancini's "Moon River" ("I'm crossing you in style . . .").

— 140 —

Compose a still life. Think of a particular object or set of objects that have some significance in their grouping and representation. What does it mean to "capture" a scene? Compose an auditory collage. Borrow musical elements in their entirety; cut and paste.

— 141 —

Good idea: whistling while you work. Bad idea: whistling while you eat. Write a song about an incident where "it seemed like a good idea at the time" applies.

— 142 —

Write a song from the underdog's perspective. Give voice to somebody usually disenfranchised. Write from the villain's perspective or the perspective of an unfamous sidekick, such as Tonto or Sancho Panza. Examples: *Grendel* by John Gardner, "Mata Hari" and "Cyrano Ballet" (both by John Gart), or "Billy the Kid" (one each by Burl Ives, Skitch Henderson, and Aaron Copeland).

— 143 —

Do you have wanderlust? Tell why or why not.

— 144 —

Is there something about you that nobody in your family understands?

Now's your chance to set them straight in a song.

— 145 —

Start with an octave, e.g., "When You Wish Upon a Star" (Ned Washington and Leigh Harline) or "Somewhere Over the Rainbow" (E.Y. "Yip" Harburg and Harold Arlen).

— 146 —

Imagine how heroes, such as Zorro, Conan the Barbarian, Batman, Amelia Earhart, Eleanor Roosevelt, Martin Luther King Jr., handle fear. Use fear and conquering fear as a theme in your writing.

— 147 —

Meeting and overcoming obstacles is the central plot in most film scripts. And guess what industry needs lots of music at those plot points?

— 148 —

Recall your first days of elementary school, junior high school, high school, college; remember your first girlfriend/boyfriend, first job, first boss. What did you tell yourself? What was terrible? What was great? Experience that fear again. How do you cope?

— 149 —

You're at your parent's grave site. What do you say?

— 150 —

You're saying good-bye to your kid, driving him or her to college.

What do you say?

— 151 —

You're at your golden wedding anniversary party. What do you say?

— 152 —

You're trying to persuade your family to move to the country (or to the city) from where they are. Extol the virtues of the other place.

— 153 —

You gotta brag. Go ahead, tell the people what's so special about you, him, her, us.

— 154 —

Testify about something you've learned. Warn somebody about the mistake they're going to make, e.g., "He Don't Love You Like I Love You" (Jerry Butler, Curtis Mayfield, and Carlton Carter), "Mamas, Don't Let Your Babies Grow Up to Be Cowboys" (Ed and Patsy Bruce).

— 155 —

You caught somebody in a lie; confront them in a song.

— 156 —

What's the song that would go best with a shimmy and sequins?

— 157 —

What's the song that would go best with a top hat and cane?

A smoky dive? A big ballroom?

— 158 —

What's the song that would go best with a ten-gallon hat?

— 159 —

Write about an unusual way of life—for example, the lion tamer's song, the pipe fitter's song, the pastry chef's song, as in Jimmy Webb's "Wichita Lineman." Write about hoboes, street people, and the unemployed; and rather than just observe their blues, find something unexpected in them to write about.

— 160 —

Birds, flowers, rivers. Connect one of these to an emotion, e.g., "The Red Tailed Hawk" by George Schroder or "River" by Bill Staines.

— 161 —

Write a song that an exercise class could work out to.

— 162 —

Put as many colors or as much color as you can into a lyric, e.g., Prince's "Raspberry Beret."

— 163 —

You visited a gypsy/palmist/card reader. What did they say?

— 164 —

Write a song about a sport. Examples: "Golf Is a Four-letter Word," "This Is the NFL" (Rolfe Wyer II and Peter Dergee), "Dropkick Me, Jesus" ("through the goalposts of life") by Paul Craft.

— 165 —

What happened "Just in Time"
(Adolph Green, Jule Styne, and Betty Comden)?

— 166 —

Write a train song, that is, a song using a "train" rhythm, like "My Baby Thinks He's a Train" by Leroy Preston.

— 167 —

Write a "cat on the keys" song and remember what they say about jazz: "There are no wrong notes in jazz."

— 168 —

Create your own Dr. Seuss character and his/her/its song.

— 169 —

What would extinct animals (a dinosaur, a dodo bird) have to say about the world as it is? What would a fictional character, such as Rip van Winkle, say?

— 170 —

Pretend you're a different age than you are and write in that voice. "All I Want for Christmas Is My Two Front Teeth" (Don Gardner).

— 171 —

What is a good lover? Friend? Buddy? Who is a good lover? Friend? Buddy? What are they like? What is a Mensch? Who is a Mensch to you?

— 172 —

Miracles never cease. Write about some everyday miracles or some "Wonders of the World." Write about magic.

— 173 —

Make distinctions among a lady, a woman, and a girl and write about them, or tell why they're the same in somebody.

— 174 —

Defend somebody who's been attacked.

— 175 —

Rewrite clichés, write from them, or write them into your song. Here are some suggestions: out of the clear blue sky, pay dearly, alive and well, in no time flat, down in the dumps, a complete disaster, my one and only, reckless abandon, eyes glued, shivers up my spine, broke my heart, racked my brain, heavy as a rock, quiet as a mouse, sharp as a tack, light as a feather, well aware, last but not least, not a care in the world, a lump in my throat, safe and sound, a rude awakening.

— 176 —

Take a song lyric that you've already written, draw a circle around each cliché, then replace each cliché with an original lyric.

— 178 —

Strip away some masks of adulthood; e.g., "Other people cannot see what I see. Whenever I look into your father's face, far behind your father's face as it is today, are all those other faces which were his. Let him laugh and I see a cellar your father does not remember and a house he does not remember and I hear in his present laughter his laughter as a child" (James Baldwin).

— 179 —

Keep a journal for a week if you haven't already. A lifetime would be good.

— 180 —

Write about a party, for a party, having a party, a ceilidh, paney-iri, a right of passage, a wake, something festive, or something that should be festive but isn't, as in "Mama Told Me Not to Come" (Randy Newman). Use the soundscape, e.g., William Carlos Williams on Bruegel's painting, "the squeal and the blare and the tweedle, the bugle and the fiddles, tipping their bellies").

— 181 —

Write the background music to a chase scene. (Fire engines and cars flying off the ends of piers are optional.)

— 182 —

What have you been avoiding? Speak up. As in that Elton John and Bernie Taupin song "Your Song" or "I'll Have to Say I Love You in a Song" by Jim Croce, this may be your chance to say what otherwise might be hard to put into words. Let songwriting make the telling *easier*.

— 183 —

Push "the little engine that could."

— 184 —

Gossip. Do a best/worst list, or tell how gossip has affected you, e.g., "I Heard It Through the Grapevine" (Norman Whitfield and Barrett Strong) or "New Kid in Town" (Glenn Frey, Don Henley, and J. D. Souther).

— 185 —

Write down the rules of formulaic commercial songwriting as you know them . . . then break them—BLAM!—one by one. Or parody them. For example, "Blah Blah Blah" (George and Ira Gershwin) was written as a protest against all the rhymes conventionally used for "moon." "Scrambled Eggs" was the original title to Paul McCartney's "Yesterday." "Achy Breaky Heart" was written after writer Don von Tress failed to get several serious, personal songs published. Write the absolute most trite, stupid song you can, using the stuff you hate the most. My personal hit list includes the rhymes "higher," "desire," and "fire." Also, I detest the phrase, "tore my heart in two."

— 186 —

Debunk some of the great laws through the ages: the world is flat, the sun revolves around the earth, underwear has to be white, nice guys finish last, your face will freeze in that position, all the good ones are taken . . .

— 187 —

Tell the history of a house or set the action in one of these rooms: bedroom, parlor, sauna, hallway, kitchen, cellar, foyer, transept, boudoir, laboratory, den, nook, attic, belfry. Back at the old corral? Back at the cave?

— 188 —

Take an article of clothing and make it emblematic of a person's experience. Examples: "High Heel Sneakers" (Robert Higginbotham), "Blue Suede Shoes" (Carl Perkins), "This Shirt" by Mary Chapin Carpenter.

— 189 —

Put a person and a flavor together, e.g., your lover and cinnamon, sassafras, ginger, apple, mango, butter. What was his/her cooking like? Where did you go and what did you eat on that picnic by the lake, after church, at the beach, at the drive-in?

— 190 —

Write a monster song for Halloween.

— 191 —

Write about a force of nature: She's a "Hurricane With Two Eyes" (Lisa Aschmann and Henry Hipkens); "Shake, Rattle, and Roll" by Charles Calhoun; or "I Feel the Earth Move" by Carole King.

— 192 —

Pay musical tribute to cartoon characters, e.g., Betty Boop, Ren and Stimpy, Scooby Doo, the seven dwarves, Daffy Duck, the Flintstones, Bullwinkle, Garfield, the Simpsons, Bugs Bunny, Snoopy.

— 193 —

Euro-pop or techno-pop music makes heavy use of synthesizers. Write something with as many samples or different synthesizer sounds as you can fit in. Write a symphony. Write a rock opera.

— 194 —

Write something for a great instrumentalist, living or dead, such as Jimi Hendrix or Liszt, to be challenged by.

— 195 —

Write the simplest song you could teach to a five-year-old.

— 196 —

Write a cheer.

— 197 —

Write an acronym.

— 198 —

Write a song for an unborn child.

— 199 —

Rewrite existing songs with one-third of the notes, then add different ones.

— 200 —

Write a song for doing laundry by hand. If you were washing clothes at the river, for instance, what would your song be?

— 201 —

What falls? Leaves fall. You fall asleep. You fall in love.
"Freefallin'" (Tom Petty)

What gives? What sways? What breaks? Group verbs that might emotionally key a song.

— 202 —

Flatter and pamper somebody verbally.

— 203 —

Write about energy and sex. Chemistry! Electricity! Wind me up. Pull my string. Big wind, cool wind, Niagara Falls, heat wave.

— 204 —

Write a song for a red letter day such as payday, getting out of jail, your class reunion, Sunday morning, Friday (TGIF), or Saturday night.

— 205 —

Write Muzak for the elevator, the roller coaster, the elephant parade, the cafeteria, the busboy, the pearl diver. If the beauty shop hair dryers had a song, what would it be? What about the five seconds of music that plays when you win a video game? Reward somebody with a little musical pat on the back.

— 206 —

Write another song for the Shakers or the Quakers or the Amish or the Luddites—people who like to keep it simple.

— 207 —

What would it mean to really serve someone? Do a mitzvah (good deed) in a song or *with* a song or talk about one in the lyrics.

— 208 —

Write down your dreams. They may contain juice for songs.

— 209 —

Write a song for each of the four directions: south, east, west, and north. Or write one song about all of them.

— 210 —

Write a chant for a ritual, e.g., a solstice celebration.

— 211 —

Games people play—what are they?

— 212 —

Comment on voices: a purr, a whine, a voice husky with emotion, a croak, a sharp exhalation of breath, a deep honeyed voice, admonitory whispers, uneasy laughter, quiet dignity, trembling with indignation. Or lilting, quavering, cold, thin, reedy, prickling, savage, passionate, resonant, unsteady, roaring, disembodied, tight, or triumphant tones.

— 213 —

Comment on smiles: a gentle smile, a tolerant smirk, an inviting smile, a flash of curiosity, a grin. Try different gestures and illustrate them musically.

— 214 —

Write a march. Sousa is full of terrific examples (also Ives and Joplin). You don't have to come down hard on the count of ONE two three four; you could syncopate it. But then it might be a ragtime march.

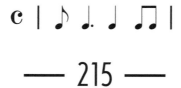

— 215 —

Write a song about unlikely, but true, love. Think of two people at total opposite ends of the social spectrum—the flower seller and the professor, the schoolteacher and the king, rival gang members—and put them together in a romantic duo. (This is the crux of most musical theater plots circa 1930-50.) Write songs to introduce the characters and further the plot and you have the beginnings of a musical. Maybe you'll want to pursue this. There's a lot of nobility in unrequited love. (See *Wicked* by Eric Schwarz based on Gregory McGuire's book.)

— 216 —

Use a song to describe or define or affirm yourself, e.g., "That'll Be Me" (Kevin Welch), "This Is Me"(Tom Shapiro and Thom McHugh), "The Way I Am" (Sonny Throckmorton), "Who I Am" (Brett James and Troy Verges).

— 217 —

Use the pace of a song to imitate the pace of sex or another event, e.g., Ravel's "Bolero" imitates the buildup (or maybe Peter Gabriel's "Sledgehammer" does).

—— 218 ——

A friend of mine, Jill Kramer, talks about the genre she calls "the sensitive rat" song, in which the main character sweetly justifies some obnoxious behavior (cheating, leaving, etc.). Some of the biggest sellers let 'em down easy. Try this out if you can't help yourself.

—— 219 ——

Write a song using a one-word title. For instance, "Faith" (Lisa Aschmann and Carol Hashe), "Physical" (Terry Shaddick and Stephen Kipner), "Anticipation" (Carly Simon), "Reunited" (Frederick Perren and Dino Fekaris), "Fame" (Dean Pitchford and Michael Gore), "Nagasaki" (Mort Dixon and Harry Warren.)

—— 220 ——

Put some sequencing in your harmony, adding interior, and moving lines in the upper registers, e.g., Herman Hupfeld's "As Time Goes By." Or use a chained suspension as in Jerome Kern's Em7 → A7 → Dmaj7 and Em9 → A7$^{\#5}$ → Dmaj9.

—— 221 ——

Feature a prominent chromatically descending bass line, like Henry Purcell's "Dido's Lament" or "Let It Be Me" by Manny Kurtz, Gilbert Silly, and Pierre Leroyer.

— 222 —

Feature a prominently ascending chromatic bass line,
e.g., 1 → ♯1dim → 2 → 5.

— 223 —

Modulate like crazy. Examples: "Lover" by Richard Rodgers
and Lorenz Hart, "The Song Is You" by Jerome Kern and Oscar
Hammerstein or "I've Never Been in Love Before" by Frank Loesser.

— 224 —

Write a tango. Write a samba. Write a cueca.
Ever tried a cha cha? A meringue?

— 225 —

Use some ethnic, exotic instruments to sweeten up your tracks and
inspire you, e.g., the Turkish tzaz, the African mbira, the Japanese koto.

— 226 —

Put together a gamelan orchestra. How about a jug band?
Get out the spoons. Hambone.

— 227 —

Parody a vocal style. Imagine somebody you'd like to have record your song and "target write" to their specifications. Put their voice, what they're likely to say, and as much of their style as possible in what you write. Some artists are particularly fun to imitate vocally (Elvis, Dylan). How about Leon Redbone?

— 228 —

Write a song for different pavilions at the World's Fair, Expo, the Olympics, etc. Does your team/town/state/country have a song yet?

— 229 —

Lead the ear to certain rhymes and then go someplace else as in "Nellie had a steamboat; the steamboat had a bell . . ."

— 230 —

Rhyme in couplets only or use double and triple syllable rhymes throughout a piece.

— 231 —

Use tons of inner rhymes. Cole Porter was a master: "Do do that voodoo that you do so well" (I've Got You Under My Skin").

— 232 —

Read the dedications, acknowledgements, and prefaces in books. Who were these people to each other? You can get some vicarious pleasure out of people expressing their gratitude and positive relationships to each other (as well as a lot of choice song ideas). Autobiographies and books containing letters are especially juicy for song ideas, particularly in the boyhood/girlhood stages of peoples' lives.

— 233 —

If you play guitar, go up the neck, using chords that keep the same basic shape of the fingers. Try different strums that you haven't before. Try different tunings. DADGAD and G tunings may restrict your choices, but they provide lots of open strings that could lead to nice Celtic-inflected melodies and fiddle tunes.

— 234 —

Write music to accompany a contra dance, or a square dance, complete with calls.

— 235 —

If you play banjo, write for different five-string or four-string frailing and plucking techniques and compare them. Imitate an old-time American folk style. If you play bass, try writing for fretted and fretless bass, standup bass, bowed bass, or cello and compare them. If you play sax or recorder, play with writing for the alto, tenor, and soprano versions of your instrument. Experiment with instruments related to yours, e.g., dulcimer, hammered dulcimer, autoharp, zither; accordion concertina, squeezebox; organ, piano, harpsichord, synthesizer.

— 236 —

Invent an "instrument" (e.g., comb and tissue paper, sticks, toilet paper rolls, rattles). Write for a kazoo. Use a mouth harp or harmonica and see where it takes you.

— 237 —

Write a subtractive song, which makes use of successively fewer and fewer words.

"Little Rabbit in the Wood" or "Under the Spreading Chestnut Tree" Or, write a song that would be fun for a mime or a clown to perform silently.

— 238 —

Somebody reminds you of somebody else. Write about déjà vu or the way your memories play tricks on you.

— 239 —

Write about going fishing.

"Baby's Goin' Fishin'," "Fishing Blues" (Henry Thomas and J. M. Williams) or "You and Me Goin' Fishin' in the Dark" (Wendy Waldman and Jim Photoglo), "Cruisin'" (Smokey Robinson), "Groovin'" (Felix Cavaliere and Eddie Brigati). Check out the scene at a bar or high school dance or the "Night Moves" (Bob Seger) afterward. Or hey, maybe just a song about fishing.

— 240 —

Use gambling metaphors, e.g., "The Joker" ("in the Deck") (Steve Miller), "I Feel Lucky" (Mary Chapin Carpenter and Don Schlitz), "Two of a Kind Workin' on a Full House" (Bobby Boyd, Warren Haynes, and Dennis Robbins), "Roll of the Dice" (Bruce Springsteen), "Aces" (Cheryl Wheeler), "Lily, Rosemary, and the Jack of Hearts" (Bob Dylan).

— 241 —

Where do you want to go when you die? Is there an afterlife? How do you want to be disposed of? Think about John Prine's "Please Don't Bury Me" or Tony Arata's "Someday I Will Lead the Parade."

— 242 —

What is perfect? Inviolate? Invincible? Sacred? True? "The best thing that ever happened to me . . ." Use superlatives to describe something. Be fulsome with someone.

— 243 —

Understate the case, as in "(You're) Just a Little in Love" (Ron Reynolds and Amanda Hunt).

— 244 —

Write a song that a modern dance troupe could choreograph, e.g., "Clockwork" (Alex de Grassi) or "On a Tightwire" (Steven Brown).

— 245 —

Write a song about a mythical beast—a gryphon, phoenix, or unicorn— or mythology, like the stories "The Golden Fleece," "The Cyclops," and "Medusa."

— 246 —

The right thing to say. What was it? When?

— 247 —

What is the funniest thing you ever saw? Heard? The saddest? The most beautiful?

— 248 —

How did your parents react to your boyfriend/girlfriend? How did you friends react? To your breakup? To your engagement? What advice did they give? (People are always chock full of advice.) Make something up if you can't remember.

— 249 —

Write a song from the perspective of a person in circumstances far removed from your own but with whom you can still identify, e. g., a Lapp, a Bedouin, a wino, a nun, a Navajo, a geisha girl, a Southern sharecropper, a coal miner, an organ grinder, a ventriloquist, a warden, an inmate, a pharaoh, a wandering Jew (not a house plant!).

— 250 —

Ask a Socratic (leading) question that you know the answer to.

Examples:
"Do I Love You?" (Cole Porter)
"Am I Blue?" (Grant Clarke and Harry Akst)

— 251 —

Change a reality premise slightly. For instance, "Twenty-Five Hours a Day" (Craig Cooper), "Eight Days a Week" (Lennon and McCartney), "We'll have one hundred and twenty babies . . ." ("Anchorage" by Michelle Shocked).

— 252 —

State the obvious. Locate yourself. For example: "Here I Am" (Tony Arata), "I'm Not Lisa," ("My name is Julie") (Jessi Colter), "And there you were" ("How Sweet It Is" by Brian Holland and Lamont Dozier).

— 253 —

You wouldn't believe the number of songs that start with, "Got up this morning" or "Sittin' here." Start with where you are. Look around. Check in with yourself. How do you feel *right now*? What's uppermost in your mind *right now*?

— 254 —

Write a zipper song. That's a song that "zips" a word or a line in and out of the rest of the existing structure. Examples: "She'll Be Comin' 'Round the Mountain," Si Kahn's "People Like You Help People Like Me Go On," or Holly Near's "Singing for Our Lives." Zipper songs are a good source of singalongs.

— 255 —

Write an additive song, e.g., "There's a Hole in the Bottom of the Sea," (trad.) "The Ladies of the Court of King Koracticus," "Whoever Shall Have Some Good Peanuts" (Cathy Fink). These are songs that tell a story serially, by adding one element at a time, summing up the action in ever-longer choruses.

— 256 —

Write a riddle song, e.g., "I Gave My Love a Cherry," "Tumbalalaika," "There Were Three Sisters." Or write in a question/answer format, e.g., "There's a Hole in My Bucket" or "Can You Count the Stars?" (Jonathan Willcocks).

— 257 —

What makes you crazy? How are you crazy?

— 258 —

Wallow.

— 259 —

Bust out.

— 260 —

You rascal, you!

— 261 —

Give yourself a good talking to.

— 262 —

Write about the radio ("Turn Your Radio On" by Albert Brumley or "I'm a Radio" by Joni Mitchell), or the television, or the news ("Dirty Laundry" by Don Henley).

— 263 —

Write for a barbershop quartet.

— 264 —

Write a madrigal. Write for a choir.

— 265 —

Write a song for three voices. Stacked bluegrass harmonies. A duet.

— 266 —

Set to music some instructions or "found poetry"; e.g., the Miranda rights, the stuff they tell you on airplanes about your oxygen mask in the overhead compartment, how to assemble a kid's toy, etc.

— 267 —

Go through Bartlett's *Familiar Quotations* or another compendium of quotable quotes and substitute "love" or "heart" for some of the other nouns. Rewrite familiar sayings or other people's song titles. For instance, "Somewhere Under the Rainbow" (Jerry Laseter, Kerry Phillips, and Scott Blackwell). Turn a phrase, e.g., "Home Is Where the Heart Aches" (Lisa Aschmann, Joel Evans, and J. D. Smith) or "The High Cost of Loving" (Hal Bynum and Dave Kirby).

— 268 —

Just for the pun of it, put some puns in your song.

"I'd rather have a bottle in front of me than a frontal lobotomy" (W. C. Fields), "If I Said You Had a Beautiful Body" ("would you hold it against me?") (David Bellamy)

And here's a verse I love from "The Swimming Song" by Loudon Wainwright III:

"This summer, I swam in a public place
And in a reservoir, to boot.
At the latter, I was informal.
At the former, I wore my suit."

— 269 —

Tell about what's possible in your relationship, e.g., "I Will" (Paul McCartney), "We Could" (Felice Bryant) or "Someday We'll Be Together" (Jackey Beavers and Johnny Bristol). Optimism in itself is a great theme in songwriting, e.g., "Rose Colored Glasses" (John Conlee and George Barber), "I Can See Clearly Now" (Johnny Nash).

— 270 —

Write about a disaster. Examples: "The Springhill Mine Disaster" (Peggy Seeger), "The Titanic" (Leadbelly), "Barrett's Privateers" (Stan Rogers), "The Wreck of the Old 97" (Fred Lewey, Charles Noell, and Henry Work), "The Wreck on the Highway" (Roy Acuff), "The Wreck of the Edmund Fitzgerald" (Gordon Lightfoot).

— 271 —

Write about a deal with the devil, e.g., "The Devil Went Down to Georgia" (Charlie Daniels) or "Shoeless Joe from Hannibal, Mo" (Jerry Ross and Richard Adler), or pick another classic folktale to retell in song. What happened to Paul Bunyan and Pecos Bill? Coyote? Silke? Loki? Anansi?

— 272 —

Modernize a hero as in "Joe Hill" (Earl Robinson and Alfred Hayes) and "Geronimo's Cadillac" (Charles John Quarto and Michael Martin Murphy).

— 273 —

Write a "before you"/"after you" scenario, e.g., ("there were birds all around, but I never heard them singing") "Till There Was You" (Meredith Willson) or ("you made me leave my happy home; you took my love and now you're gone") "Since I Fell for You" (Buddy Johnson). People change, sometimes everything, for each other.

— 274 —

Have you ever written a rockabilly tune? Everybody thinks of Elvis, but how about Carl Perkins, Jerry Lee Lewis, or Gene Vincent?

— 275 —

How about a conjunto tune, or a Tex-Mex tune?

How about inflecting a song in English with a Latin influence, e.g., "Living la Vida Loca" (Ricky Martin and Desmond Childs). Desmond is a very successful writer/producer who is American but was raised by Cubanos.

— 276 —

Start the chorus right *on* the downbeat, e.g., "Blue Skies" ("smiling at me") (Irving Berlin), "Roll Out the Barrel" (Vaclav Zeman, Jaromir Vejvoda, Wladimir Timm, and Lew Brown).

— 277 —

Look up movies in production in *The Hollywood Reporter* or a similar trade magazine and see if you can get in on the ground floor by writing something appropriate for them; something somebody's working on may not have the music yet. Or write what ought to be the sequel to existing shows and themes, the trailer music, etc.

— 278 —

Make a long story short.

— 279 —

Make a list of dos and don'ts:

"Don't Fence Me In" (Cole Porter)
"Don't Let Your Deal Go Down" (Charlie Poole)
"Ruby, Don't Take Your Love to Town" (Mel Tillis)
"Don't Be Cruel" (Otis Blackwell)
"Love Me Like You Used To" (Paul Davis and Bobby Emmons)
"Mind Your Own Business" (Hank Williams)
"Move It on Over" (Hank Williams)
"Act Naturally" (Voni Morrison and Johnny Russell)
"Build Me Up" (John Colla and Hugh Clegg)
"Do That to Me One More Time" (Toni Tennille)
"Run to Me" (Barry, Maurice, and Robin Gibb)

— 280 —

Put a stop or sudden rest in a rhythm. Use a vocal that's not singing like in "Pretty Woman" when Roy Orbison growls or the "Ahoo! Ahoo!" in "Werewolves of London" (Warren Zevon). Or talk part of your melody, e.g., "Take This Job and Shove It" (David Allan Coe) or "Ragtime Cowboy Joe" (Lewis Muir and Hubert Arnold).

— 281 —

Write new melodies over these strong progressions:

1 → 5 → 1,

1 → 6mi → 2mi → 5 → 1,

1 → 3mi → 6mi → 2mi → 5 → 1

— 282 —

Write about being young, e.g., "Young Blood" (Jerry Leiber, Doc Pomus, and Mike Stoller) or ("young hearts, be free tonight") "Young Turks" by Rod Stewart. Does the future beckon to you? Maybe you're "Forever Young" (Bob Dylan).

— 283 —

Write a song with "yes," "no," or "maybe" in the title.

— 284 —

Go for the absolutes. Finish these phrases:

I never _____.

I only _____.

I always _____.

I'm gonna _____.

I still _____.

Everything _____.

Nothing _____.

— 285 —

J'accuse. Start with "you." Examples: "You" (Tom Snow), "You Ain't Seen Nothin' Yet" (Randy Bachman), "You Don't Have to Be a Baby to Cry" (Bob Merrill and Terry Shand), "You Can't Hurry Love" (Eddie Holland, Lamont Dozier, and Brian Holland), "You Are the Sunshine of My Life" (Stevie Wonder). As you can see, starting like this can give rise to either a really intimate or really general, universal lyric.

— 286 —

Write about money, affluence, or lack of same. Philosophize. Is it everything? Is it nothing? How much does it matter? For instance, "Big Spender" (Dorothy Fields and Cy Coleman), "Forever in Blue Jeans" (Neil Diamond and Richard Bennett), "Flower Lady" (Phil Ochs), "Pocket Full of Gold" (Vince Gill).

— 287 —

Go to the movies. John Hartford tells the story of having written "Gentle on My Mind"—the most-often played song in America— after having seen *Dr. Zhivago*.

— 288 —

Write a song somebody could do a hula to. Write with Hawaiian guitar or pedal steel in mind. How about steel drums?

— 289 —

Write a song using dobro or sympathetic strings added, a slide on the guitar, or some other specialty attachment to an instrument.

— 290 —

Write a song about "one" of something. Examples: "One Trick Pony" (Paul Simon), "One Mint Julep" (Rudolph Toombs), "One More Try" (Bobby Gene Hall, Jr. and Raymond Simpson), "One Tin Soldier" (Dennis Lambert and Brian Potter), "One of These Nights" (Don Henley and Glenn Frey), "You Are the One" (Carroll Carroll and John Scott Trotter). Write about how somebody or something is unique. Write about how somebody or something is "just one more" in a line or a bunch.

— 291 —

Make up a dance and a song to go with it. "Mashed Potatoes," "The Watusi," "The Twist," and "Cotton-Eyed Joe" were once just a gleam in some songwriter's eye. And what about "Walk Like an Egyptian" (Liam Sternberg), "Loco-motion" (Carole King and Gerry Goffin), ("And they'll be dancin' . . . dancin' in Chicago . . . down in New Orleans . . .") from "Dancing in the Street" by Marvin Gaye, William Stevenson, and Ivy George Hunter.

— 292 —

What did you two lovebirds fight about? Aren't you sorry now?

— 293 —

A lifetime of longing. If only . . . If you had it to do over . . .

Promises. Fulfilled. Unfulfilled. Explore your regrets.
But for godsakes, don't stay there!

— 294 —

Flagellate yourself. Hey, it was good enough for the plague years.
Crawl a little. For instance, ("I'll be") "Working My Way Back to You"
(Sandy Linzer and Denny Randell), ("I'd get") "Down on My Knees"
(Beth Nielsen Chapman), "Guilty" (Randy Newman), "Sorry Seems to
Be the Hardest Word" (Elton John), "Love Has No Pride" (Eric Kaz).

— 295 —

Speak for more than yourself; use first person plural.

"We Are the World" (Lionel Richie and Michael Jackson), "We Belong" (Eric
Lowen and Dan Navarro), "We Shall Overcome," "We Can Work It Out" (John
Lennon and Paul McCartney), "We Will Rock You" (Brian May). Get big and
anthemic, e.g., "Un Mundo" by Stephen Stills.

— 296 —

Use the telephone as a lyrical device. For instance, "Operator" was a
title used by the Grateful Dead, the Manhattan Transfer, and
Jim Croce, to name a few. Lately there have been lots of telephone

ring tones, and there's even a musical called *Bells Are Ringing* (Jule Styne, Adolph Green, and Betty Comden). When will faxes and e-mail start cropping up in lyrics? Or how about doorbells? Doors? Windows? Fences? Gates? The postal service? Maybe you have some feelings associated with them.

— 297 —

Ask for help in a song—"Help" (Lennon and McCartney), "Help Me" (Joni Mitchell), "Help Me Make It Through the Night" (Kris Kristofferson), "Help Me, Rhonda" (Mike Love and Brian Wilson)—or offer it—"Help on the Way" (Robert Hunter and Jerry Garcia)—or just talk about that feeling—"Helpless" (Neil Young), "Helpless Heart" (Paul Brady), "I Need You to Turn To" (Elton John and Bernie Taupin).

— 298 —

What will never change, no matter what?

— 299 —

Pick a number. A popular one to write about is the number two, e.g., "Two Doors Down" (Dolly Parton), "Two Sides" (Scott Davis), "Two Hearts" (Bruce Springsteen), "Two Out of Three Ain't Bad" (Jim Steinman). If you are part of a dyad, you could write about "Us" (Burt Bacharach and Bobby Russell) or "Our House" (Graham Nash), etc. Does the number two make you feel divided and schizophrenic or cozy and comfortable in your relationship?

— 300 —

Use "so" or "very" or "all" in a song title. Get emphatic.

— 301 —

Use the diminutive, e.g., "Little . . ." "Baby . . ." "Honey . . ." "Darlin' . . ." "Sugar . . ." "Child . . ." Ooh! What a way to address somebody!

— 302 —

Question reality, e.g., "Can This Be Real?" (Janice Huston, Lee Hutson, and Michael Hawkins), "This Can't Be Love" (Rodgers and Hart). Question your dream, e.g., "Do I Love You Because You're Beautiful?" ("or are you beautiful because I love you") (Rodgers and Hammerstein). Tackle the topic of imagination itself, e.g., "Impossible" from the musical *Cinderella* (also by Rodgers and Hammerstein): "And because these daft and dewy-eyed dopes keep building up impossible hopes, impossible things are happening every day." My sentiments *exactly*!

— 303 —

Ask why or where or what. When you're at your wits end, admit it. When you're lonesome, admit it. Songs are great vehicles for this kind of soul searching.

— 304 —

Marvel. "What a Wonderful World!" (Sam Cooke, Herb Alpert, Lou Adler), "Thank God I'm a Country Boy!" (John Denver).

— 305 —

Illness and infatuation have often been compared. Complain about your ailments. Do you have a "Fever" (John Davenport and Eddie Cooley)? A "Lovebug" (Curtis Wayne and Wayne Kemp)?

— 306 —

Notice how the grass is always greener? Write about envy, greed, invidious comparisons, e.g., "Jesse's Girl" (Rick Springfield), "What's He Got That I Ain't Got?" (Peter McCann), "How Come We're Always Looking?" (Roger Fennings, Charles Herndon, and Chip Raines), "Mom Always Liked You Best" (Tommy Smothers).

— 307 —

Persuade somebody to go to bed with you. No! No! In a *song*, silly!

— 308 —

Write a song that has a large descending interval at the beginning of the chorus and then goes back up, e.g., Crowded House's

("Hey now, hey now,") "Don't Dream It's Over" (Neil Finn) or Peter Cetera's "Next Time I Fall" (in love").

— 309 —

Write a song that has some sixteenth notes in it.

How about some four-count rests? A fermata?

— 310 —

Play with waltz time. Try writing one of each:

Viennese (a big downbeat on 1)
Cajun (pushing beat 2 early)
Jazz waltz (emphasizing all 3 beats)

— 311 —

Bless your heart, have you written your saint's day songs yet? St. Valentine's Day? St. Nick's? How about St. Swithin's Day? And it's only fair to mention the patron saint of travelers when you're traveling. How about mentioning St. Peter at the Pearly Gates? Uh . . . St. James' infirmary?

— 312 —

The things we do for love! Write about something you'd roll your eyes or shake your head about if you were older and wiser.

— 313 —

The two manmade items visible from space, so say the astronauts, are the pyramids and the Great Wall of China. Suppose *you* were to write and make a huge, lasting impression. Strive to make something "stick out" in the auditory landscape, *way* out.

— 314 —

Write a song that goes outside the range of your own singing voice.

— 315 —

Write a song regarding wrestling.

— 316 —

Write a song of exultation, a breakthrough, a quest succeeding, a triumphant return.

— 317 —

Finish this phrase: Isn't it ironic that _____.

— 318 —

She's/he's hysterical. ("She's a") "Maniac" (Michael Sembello), "Jam Up and Jelly Tight" (Tommy Roe) "Blinded by the Light" (Bruce Springsteen), a monster, a "Wild Thing" (Chip Taylor), "Barney Jekyll and Bubba Hyde" (Craig Wiseman and Gene Nelson). What is the thing this person has turned into and why? On the dance floor? At a party? In bed? When they take off their shoes? When they put on their "Dancin' Shoes" (Carl Storie), does "Baby Likes to Rock It" like the Tractors? Or what?

— 319 —

Try doo wop style. That is, write a triplet rhythm, drag on the count of 1, backbeat on 2 and 4: ONE and two and three and ONE. Examples: "This Boy" (Lennon and McCartney), "Tell It Like It Is" (George Davis and Lee Diamond), "Earth Angel" (Curtis Williams, Gaynel Hodge, and Jesse Belvin).

— 320 —

Play variations on 1 6 2 5 1, with passing tones. In the key of C, for instance: C Am Dm G C → C Cmaj7 Amin9 Dm$^{\#11}$ G$^{\flat 9}$ Cmaj9. In other words, fancy up your chords.

— 321 —

Write on cultures in conflict/contact, e.g., "Ebony and Ivory" (Paul McCartney), "A Midnight Girl in a Sunset Town" (Don Schlitz), "All I Want to Be Is Understood" (Michael O'Hara, Denise Rich, and Mary Unobsky).

— 322 —

"When you're down and troubled, and you need a helping hand . . ." Console somebody. "You've Got a Friend" by Carole King is a good example of this type of song.

— 323 —

Yeah . . . serenity . . . I got your serenity right here, buddy. Write a song that shows 'em just how ticked off you are. Or comment on a song that's already out there that makes you mad, e.g., "God Didn't Make Honky Tonk Angels" (Jay Miller), "I Wish I Had a Job to Shove" (Billy Ray Reynolds and Ronnie Rogers).

— 324 —

Rue your hangover in a song, i.e., "Wasn't That a Party?" (Tom Paxton), "Too Much Tequila" (Dave Burgess), or write about a party going awry ("we've been invited to") "Henrietta's Wedding" ("we can't tell when or where it will be . . .") (Josef Marais and Gideon Fagan).

— 325 —

Write about the aging or physical imperfection of somebody as if it's unrelated to who they are as a person, e.g., "I'm a Little Cookie" (Larry Penn), "Walking on My Wheels" (Mark Cohen), "Forever and Ever, Amen" (Paul Overstreet and Don Schlitz).

— 326 —

Use the concept of shadows and light in a lyric. Clouds. Smoke, Fog, Candles.

— 327 —

Use some diminished chords. Get "spooky."

— 328 —

Use some augmented chords. Get "churchy."

— 329 —

Write a song for the child in your life. The child inside of you. Uh, the teenager with raging hormones?

— 330 —

Write a song for or on marimba, vibes, xylophone, or a related instrument. Play with a fork on glasses filled with various amounts of water. (If you have crystal goblets, so much the better. Lucky you!)

— 331 —

What did/do people tell you for your own good? Did/do you listen?

— 332 —

"Truckin'." If there's a profession that can use some accompanying music, that's got to be one of them, for example, "Drivin' My Life Away" (Eddie Rabbitt).

— 333 —

Write some muddy-sounding tracks for a garage band or grunge rock, etc. Feature lead guitar to the *hilt*.

— 334 —

Write a talking blues, like Woody Guthrie's "Dust Bowl Blues."

— 335 —

A corny song wouldn't be so bad, now, would it?
It would just be . . . well . . . corny.

— 336 —

Take the highest note in your piece and ramp up to it and away from it.
Build a mountain in the dead center of your piece.

— 337 —

Okay, okay, it's the moon's turn.
(Nobody's ever written about the moon, have they?)

— 338 —

Write a Christmas/Chanukah/Kwanza/winter solstice song. Write a carol.

— 339 —

Write about an ecology issue; teach kids about recycling, etc.
Examples: Robert Palmer added new verses to Marvin Gaye's "What's
Going On?" Mannheim Steamroller's soundtrack *Saving the Wildlife*
is about whales, lions, pandas, penguins, etc. No dearth of concerns
or topics here: acid rain, rain forest logging, etc. Some records are
devoted to this topic, like Bill Oliver's album entitled "Don't Leave
the Water Running When you Wash the Dog."

— 340 —

Take some historical scenario that moves you and explore what it must have been like, e.g., "The Journals of Susannah Moody" by Margaret Atwood or "Solitary Hero" by Carol Elliott and Alice Randall.

— 341 —

Sick, very sick. What does your sick sense of humor tell you? Maybe Weird Al Yankovic or Tom Lehrer lurks inside you. (Ray Stevens? Martin Mull? Thank God for sick minds!)

— 342 —

Lower the limbo stick. (Make the game harder for yourself. Up the ante.)

— 343 —

Think about a topic and cluster vocabulary around it.

For example, regarding the parts of a castle, we have: the *bailey* (courtyard) walls, the *keep* (main house), the *great hall* (main room in the main house), a *drawbridge* over the moat, *parapets* (low walls along the top), *corbels* (stone brackets supporting the parapets), *machicolations* (holes in the parapets), *barbican* (forward gate before the *portcullis* or main gate), *postern* (back gate), *armory*, *gatehouse*, etc. Now you're closer to writing a song titled "A Man's Home" (Sheldon Harnick), "Castles in the Air" (Don McLean), "Castles in Spain," or "King of My Heart." Now, admittedly, some of these words don't sing very well. But if you get into most any topic, there will be specialized vocabulary to give you good, detailed pictures of it. Some of these more exact words will be the very thing to spice up your song. So, since we've got this list, how about it? Write a song about the king or princess or how defended somebody or something is, or how distant, or how fairy tale, or how grand.

— 344 —

Write a spiritually relevant story.

— 345 —

As Joseph Campbell said, "Follow your bliss." What else is there? Tell about your bliss. Has it always been this way?

— 346 —

Write about the passage of time. What are you *certain* of?

— 347 —

Finish these:

I'm not one to preach, but _____.
You've got to _____.
If you just _____.
All you have to do is _____.

— 348 —

What would you take to a desert island? And who?

— 349 —

Finish this thought: When you opened the door _____.

— 350 —

Write guidelines for kissing frogs or for getting out of the swamp.

— 351 —

There is no place you need to be going to right now. You're home.
Think about the experience, even if it just means connecting to the
ownership of your own body and your own life.

— 352 —

Finish this phrase: If I had the power, I'd _____.

— 353 —

You're losing control. How does it feel?
You're surrendering.
How does it feel?

— 354 —

Write a song for the massage table or the hot tub. Here are some examples to get you started: "Tenkuu" and "Silk Road" (both by Kitaro), "Dancing with the Lion" (Andreas Vollenweider), *Concert for the Earth* (Paul Winter), "Ancient Echoes" (Steve Halpern and Georgia Kelly), *Spectrum Suite* (Steve Halpern), "Birds of Paradise" and "Seapeace" (both by Georgia Kelly), *Poets and Angels* and *Nouveau Flamenco* (both by Ottmar Liebert).

— 355 —

Think about how you met him/her. Paint a picture, recapture the moment. Did you decide something or did it happen *to* you? Choices. Destiny. What *is* it? Example: "It Had to Be You" (Gus Kahn and Isham Jones).

— 356 —

Essential. Desirable. What's the difference? Or are they the same thing? What are you looking for that you must have, can't live without? What do you consider a luxury?

— 357 —

Using parallel 2nds or 4ths, make an oriental-sounding melody.

— 358 —

Ask a good question, like "How will I know?"

— 359 —

Take a title by a classical composer, such as Nocturne in E-flat (Chopin), Mass in C Minor (Mozart), Toccata and Fugue in D (Bach). They accomplish something in a certain key for that composer. Get into that key and try to let the very same title bring you to a different conception of the music that goes with it. A little night music? No problem! Name a key.

— 360 —

Go bananas. Milkshake. "Coconut" (as in "you put the lime in the . . .") (Harry Nilsson). Write about food. My personal favorites are songs about potatoes.

— 361 —

Rouse us, e.g., Mongo Santa Marie and his African-Cuban band. Use bagpipes, tin whistles, trumpets. Do your own version of reveille. What gets you going in the morning besides coffee?

— 362 —

Write naked. That's right, starkers. In the buff. Sing in the shower, too.

— 363 —

Get dirty. Here are some suggestions: Go down to the river or turn the hose on some dirt. Make mud pies. Mud wrestle. Finger paint. What does this have to do with songwriting? Well, everything. Everything to do with getting in touch with your playful, childlike self. Break loose. Have fun, that's what.

— 364 —

Practice putting the hook in different places in your chorus. Write a doughnut. A doughnut has the hook in the first and last lines of the chorus. This is very common in Nashville writing. Examples: Wayland Holyfield and Bob House's "Could I Have This Dance" ("for the rest of my life?") Or Bob Regan and Casey Kelly's "Soon." In a four-line cho-rus, try the following: Give lines 1 and 3 the same hook; 2 and 4 have different lines, e.g., "The Way It Is" by Bruce Hornsby. Or keep the hook in the first half of each line. "Fame" (Dean Pitchford and Michael Gore) or "She's Gone" (Daryl Hall and John Oates)

— 365 —

Pick up your dirty socks and put them in the hamper. Throw away that empty pizza box. If I sound like a mother, well, I am one; but that's not the point. Sometimes your creativity is blocked by clutter. If you create a little order around you before you begin, you might be pleasantly surprised. Do some obsessive thing, like sharpen all your pencils and line them up in order of size. Study which one has the most lead or which one is the sharpest. By all means, use your *favorite* one!

— 366 —

Imagine you're 16. Imagine you're 45. Imagine you're 101. Oy! Imagine you're 2.

— 367 —

Artist's autobiographies, besides being generally inspiring, have cool titles with great advice in them. For example: Etta James' *Rage to Survive*, Sammy Davis Jr.'s *Yes I Can*, Shirley MacLaine's *Out On a Limb* and *Dancing in the Light*. Or Richard Feynman's two-volume autobiography, *Surely You're Joking, Mr. Feynman* and *What Do You Care What Other People Think?*

— 368 —

Think like a cloud. You are a cloud.

— 369 —

I want to write a national anthem for grizzly bears. The color purple, the planet Xenon, and my navel are things I constantly think about. I wear a spaghetti colander on my head when I'm in this mood. I go to the laundromat in my zirconium hat . . . and . . . receive . . . signals . . . Get it? Act weird. It isn't acting if you are—weird.

— 370 —

Vanilla? You don't know from vanilla.

— 371 —

If you haven't written lyrics first and melody second, do that. If you haven't written melody first and lyrics second, do that. Do the opposite of your normal writing process.

— 372 —

"9 to 5" (Dolly Parton), "Nightshift" (Walter Orange and Dennis Lambert), "She Works Hard for the Money" (Donna Summer), "Living for the City" (Stevie Wonder), "Morning Train (Nine to Five)" (Sheena Easton), "Car Wash" (Norman Whitfield).

You get the idea. Let your work work for you. Sure, gripe about it. Why not? You're not on company tine.

— 373 —

Use the command form and make it active in a title: "Jump!" (Curtis Mayfield or Van Halen), "Shout!" (Isley Brothers).

— 374 —

Play dress up. Boots. Feather boa. Epaulettes. Shades.

— 375 —

Whine. Beg. Plead for mercy. Cajole. Con. Examples: "Good Mornin', Judge" (Wynonie Harris), "Officer Krupke" (Leonard Bernstein), ("Sarge, I'm only eighteen . . .") "Draft Dodger Rag" by Phil Ochs.

— 376 —

Assure somebody of your friendship, e.g., "That's What Friends Are For" (Burt Bacharach and Carole Bayer Sager). ("You can count on me") "Count on My Love" (Jesse Barish).

— 377 —

Assure somebody of your loyalty and devotion, e.g., "You Are Every Woman in the World to Me" (Dominic King and Frank Musker), "I Only Have Eyes for You" (Harry Warren and Al Dubin).

— 378 —

Get coy. "Do You Think I'm Sexy?" (Rod Stewart), ("it's the") "Right Time of the Night" (Peter McCann).

— 379 —

Probe your motivations. To get paid? To get laid? To show off? To praise God? To make 'em dance. To make 'em cry. To exorcise some demons.

To shed some light. Find out more about your intentions. They'll crop up in your music anyhow, guaranteed.

— 380 —

Focus on a single disturbing or wonderful word event, e.g., "The Night They Drove Old Dixie Down" (Robbie Robertson), "The Night Chicago Died" (Lionel Stitcher and Pete Callander). To refresh your memory, here are some shockers: Tienanmen Square; the collapse of the Berlin Wall; the Exxon *Valdez*; the shoot-out in Waco, Texas; the Oklahoma City bombing; the unibomber; the exodus from Albania; the Trail of Tears.

— 381 —

Write a biography for a real person, e.g., "Vincent" (Don McLean) about Vincent van Gogh or "Candle in the Wind" (Elton John) about Marilyn Monroe.

— 382 —

Here's a plot: Friends turn into lovers, e.g., "Friends and Lovers" by Paul Gordon and Jay Gruska. Here's another plot: Lovers turn into friends, e.g., "I Will Always Love You" by Dolly Parton.

— 383 —

"Tonight, I Celebrate My Love for You" (Michael Masser and Gerry Goffin). Find a way to do this in a song.

— 384 —

Write a biography for an imaginary person, e.g., "Eleanor Rigby" (Lennon and McCartney).

— 385 —

"Honey" (Bobby Goldsboro), "Shake, Sugaree" (Elizabeth Cotton), "Sugartime" (Charlie Phillips and Odis Echols, Jr.), "Sugar, Sugar" (Jeff Barry and Any Kim), "Sugartown" (Lee Hazelwood), "Sweet Magnolia Blossom" (Billy Crash Craddock), "My Sweet Lord" (George Harrison). Get the picture? It's gotta be *sweet* to spend time with that person.

— 386 —

Play with the spelling of a word, e.g., "There's No 'U' in Tennessee," "The Last Word in Jesus Is 'Us'."

— 387 —

Write a song that's in a minor key in the verse, major in the chorus. Then write a song that's in a major key in the verse, minor in the chorus.

— 388 —

Play with "harmonic rhythm" (i.e., how fast the chords change in your song). Don't have chords always changing at the same rate. Varying this element doesn't need to affect the overall rhythmic structure.

— 389 —

Ever write Dixieland music? Big band style (a thirty-two bar intro, sixteen-bar verses, and a sixteen or thirty-two bar chorus)? How about a piano rag? It's fun to imitate vintage styles. How about a crooner? A torch-style ballad?

— 390 —

Take different "thin sections" of a setting. Tell about the thinnest sliver of time. Have your story take place in a split second. Over a lifetime. Over generations. Over eons.

— 391 —

Men! Women! Can't live with 'em, can't live without 'em. Duke it out with the opposite sex in a lyric. How are they so different? Or are they? How do you know/enjoy/resent your gender? What are some things you do on a regular basis that are typically masculine/feminine? What are some things you do on a regular basis that are atypical of your gender?

— 392 —

Dry. Cool. Wet. Soft. Thorny. Play with textures and sounds together. Have you got synesthesia? Do you hear colors? Fabrics?

— 393 —

Write a ballet for kids. Examples: *Peter and the Wolf* (Sergei Prokofiev), *The Nutcracker* (Peter Tchaikovsky), *Hansel and Gretel*

(Engelbert Humperdinck), *Sleeping Beauty* (Igor Stravinsky and Peter Tchaikovsky). How about a ballet of *E. T., Star Wars, Indiana Jones, Spider Man, Ratatouille*, or some other popular kid's story? How about music for ice skating tournaments or gymnastics routines?

— 394 —

Some famous composers left unfinished work. For instance, Symphony No. 8 in B Minor by Franz Schubert was never finished. Maybe you could write the next movement for him.

— 395 —

Regarding the pulse of music: People walk about two steps per second. A brisk walk is about 130 steps per minute, and 110 steps per minute is ambling. Feel how music at your walking tempo, your breathing rhythm, and your varying heart rate can be used to express (or manipulate) emotion.

396

Try writing with a stop watch or minute minder. Race yourself. Do stream of consciousness writing in five-minute bursts. Write with a set duration in mind, the way jingle writers do. Write a thirty-second spot, a sixty-second spot, or a song that clocks in at exactly three minutes.

— 397 —

Tap something. Cause something to vibrate.

Here are some things to drum on: pots and pans, garbage can lids, plastic buckets, empty jars and bottles, fence posts, screens, grates, anything corrugated, stop signs, umbrellas, lampshades, steel bridges, suspension cables, lamp posts, awnings, tents, walls, doors, window. I got most of this list from W. A. Mathieu, but I find, in my own life, that spoons, toothbrushes and drinking glasses, coffee cans, and slapping my lap are my drum choices . . . Oh, and the shower head microphone . . . Ever try just making mouth noises? Pops, clicks, whistles. Underwater gargling. (Hey, Handel isn't the only one who writes "water music"!) Singing into a toilet paper roll is using an inexpensive reverb unit; an empty water cooler jug makes a mighty fine delay unit, too. Ever tried pantyhose/coat hanger microphone screens? See? The tools of your trade are *everywhere.*

— 398 —

What music should they play at your graduation? Your bar mitzvah?
Your confirmation? Your induction? Uh . . . your coronation?
Do you require, like Tchaikovsky's "1812 Overture" over
"La Marseillaise," a few discreet cannons?

— 399 —

Say "please" (it's the magic word, isn't it?) and "thank you," e.g., "Baby,
Please Don't Go" (Big Joe Williams), "Please Stay" (Burt Bacharach and
Bob Hilliard), "Please Send Me Someone to Love" (Percy Mayfield),
"Please, Please Me" (Lennon and McCartney), "Please, Mr. Postman"
(Brian Holland, Robert Bateman, and Freddie Gorman).

— 400 —

"I Told You So" (David Sanborn and Hiram Bullock);
"I Told You Once" (Jerry Irby).

I *told* you. So, what is it again that we can't get through our thick skulls?
Do tell.

— 401 —

Make fun of a dialect, e.g., "Josephine, Please No Lean on the Bell"
(Ed Nelson, Harry Pease, and Robert Leonard) popularized by Eddie
Cantor in the "roaring" forties.

— 402 —

If you're going to be down in a song, take us *way* down, e.g., Doug
Stone's "I'd Be Better Off (In a Pine Box)" or Randy Newman's "I Think
It's Going to Rain Today." Many writers owe Leonard Cohen a lot of
gratitude for showing them where their veins are located.

— 403 —

Landmarks . . . In the year I was born . . . What happened? Find out. Or
find out who else had a birthday and write about them. For example,
Cheryl Wheeler has a song about the year that the Yellow Cab Company
was founded. Mary Chapin Carpenter has a song about Haley's comet.

— 404 —

Finish this phrase: Ain't nothin' wrong with me that a little
_____won't cure. (What about snake oil, lovin' . . .)

— 405 —

In an otherwise 1 4 5 tune, try this traditional but cool progression: 1
→ 4$^{\flat}$7 → 5 as in "Salt Creek," "Red Haired Boy," and "Old Joe Clark."

— 406 —

Start your song going up a major sixth—"My Bonny Lies Over the
Ocean"—or going down a major sixth—"Nobody Knows the Trouble
I've Seen." Try descending with a major third, e.g., "Swing Low, Sweet
Chariot." Get big and brave with the starts you make.

— 407 —

A.J. and Sean Breen told me that this idea was Brian Eno's: Get three
envelopes and several index cards. On each envelope, write either
"style," "key," or "theme." Then write ideas on the cards that fall under
these categories. Put the appropriate cards into each envelope. Draw
one card from each envelope and write the resulting combination. Or
keep a card file and pull out one of these cars at random.

— 408 —

Do whatever you just did in reverse. Decide to do the idea you threw away last. Remove the last element you added. Don't fix the last mistake you made.

— 409 —

Celebrate someone's beauty, e.g., "You Are So Beautiful" by Billy Preston and Bruce Fisher. (Joe Cocker *cries* on the recording of that song.) John Lennon wrote "Julia" for his mother, and he cries on that recording, too Maybe you can find somebody or something that makes you cry because they're so beautiful. Those would be good tears . . . and good songs, too.

— 410 —

Finish these phrases:

Why, I oughta _____.
Don't you think it's time we _____?
Especially when _____.
Baby, please _____.
You'll be _____.
The minute I _____.
I just want to _____.
Go on and _____.
It's still _____.
Rockin' and a _____.
Everybody _____.
Don't you _____.
It's the _____.

We can _____.
Where do _____?
Love is _____.
You give me _____.
It's too late for _____.
People say _____.
Only a fool would _____.
All because _____.
Remember the night we _____?
It was almost _____.
For the first time, I _____.
Here is _____.
What a way to _____.
Whenever we're together _____.
I miss _____.
How I wish _____.
We weren't even _____.

— 411 —

What will you wear and what kind of car will you drive when you have your big hit song? What will your new friends and relatives be called? "And to my cousin Alfred, who said I'd never mention him in my will . . . "Hi, Alfred!"

— 412 —

"The Duke of Earl" (Eugene Dixon, Bernice Williams, and Earl Edwards), "The Duke of Dubuque" (Billy Faber, Janus Marchant, and Royal Lawrence), "The Sultans of Swing" (Mark Knopfler). Maybe you know somebody who likes to strut their stuff. Maybe they're nobility or royalty or just a royal pain. Maybe like Paul Simon's Speedo in "Was a Sunny Day" ("but his Christian name was Mr. Earl"), they just expect to be treated that way. My favorite song in this line of thinking is Don Henry's ("That's") "Mr. God" ("to you!").

— 413 —

Try writing in notation. Make lead sheets part of your writing process. Use manuscripts to help you visualize your melody. Try the latest manuscripting software or something really bizarre, like lute tablature. Put a light show together.

— 414 —

Write a raga, using quarter tones. Music for a muezzin, the Feast of Ramadan, etc.

— 415 —

Start your story in some unlikely location. How about the swamp? Examples: ("Jeremiah was a bullfrog") "Joy to the World" (Hoyt Axton), "Born on the Bayou" (John Fogerty), "Blue Bayou" (Roy Orbison), "Polk Salad Annie" (Tony Joe White). Tenements, dives, jungles, bars, dens of iniquity, and places of ill repute . . . You wouldn't want to take your mama to meet your "Private Dancer" (Mark Knopfler) or "Louise" (Paul Siebel), but you probably wouldn't mind if everybody else did (in a song). Songs are great ways to muckrake (or go slumming).

— 416 —

"Happiness Is a Thing Called Joe" (E. Y. "Yip" Harburg and Harold Arlen)
"Happiness Is a Warm Gun" (Lennon and McCartney)

Define happiness. Here are some people who have written songs to the title "Happy": Dick Seigel, George Michael, Mick Jagger and Keith Richards, William Bell, and Michel Legrand. Maybe you could add to their number. "Don't Worry, Be Happy!" (Bobby McFerrin).

— 417 —

Incite a jam session. Start a séance. Fill a punch bowl. Inaugurate a pillow fight. Cheer a football team. Break out a keg. Launch a ship.

— 418 —

Imagine some real or imaginary conflagrations. What's burning up? The obvious cliché is bridges. But there's also "Burning My Old Rowboat" (Larry Tagg).

— 419 —

What have you always wanted to write a song about but haven't yet?

— 420 —

Write a nostalgia piece. A plant can't put down its roots if it's always moving. Most of us don't know our neighbors the way our parents and grandparents knew theirs. What have we lost in our mobile society? What else?

— 421 —

Write a song about angels.

— 422 —

Put the ending first. Swap first and second verses. Uh . . . stand on your head? Yoga is a reliable day starter. Vary your work habits. Write at a different time of day than you have before. Shoehorn some time in on a weekly basis for your writing.

— 423 —

What are you in danger of becoming?
Doing? Having? Running away from?

— 424 —

Regarding unfinished business and/or moving on, finish these phrases:

I never got over _____.
I still try to _____.

You're the reason _____.
I wish I could tell you _____.
How can I _____.
Except for _____.
Until today _____.
I'll never forget _____.
By now I should _____.
Every so often I _____.
No matter where I go _____.
I guess it wasn't _____.
Sometimes you just have to _____.
But when it's all said and done _____.

— 425 —

Use a bass line to walk down in this (hip) progression: $1 \rightarrow \flat7 \rightarrow \flat6 \rightarrow 5$, like:

"Hit the Road, Jack" (Ray Charles)
"Stray Cat Strut" (Brian Setzer)
"Steppin' Out with My Baby" (Irving Berlin)
"Sixteen Tons" (Merle Travis)

— 426 —

Waterways I have known. Snow. Rain.
Rivers I have crossed. Seas I have sailed.

— 427 —

And we weren't even *in* that mood! Surprise us.

— 428 —

That's ridiculous! Absurd! Surreal! Comical! Out of the *question*.

— 429 —

Oranges and apples. What *can't* you compare?

— 430 —

The last thing that I'd ever do is _____.

— 431 —

How could you prove you love somebody? *Is* there any way?

— 432 —

Make a list of intentions. What do you value most?
What will "stay with you" 'til the end?

— 433 —

Capture the way something moves: a belly dancer, a snake,
a carousel full of children.

— 434 —

Sit still and listen. Look up at the sky and depict clouds, birds, shafts of sunlight, treetops, rooftops, the lines of airplane exhaust or the things they remind you of.

— 435 —

Investigate the darker side of Miss Goody Two Shoes.

— 436 —

It's my boo-hoo-birth-hic-day . . . waaah!

"Happy Birthday, Dear Heartache" (Mack David and Archie Jordan), "Happy Birthday, Darlin'" (Harland Howard), "Sixteen Candles" (Luther Dixon and Allyson Khent), "Forty-Five Years" (Stan Rogers). Put a little pathos into this occasion marking your advancing years. After all, you're the *only* one who's ever had a blue birthday, right?

— 437 —

Get your song criticized. Get turned down by a record label, an artist, a producer, or a publisher. Watch the GRAMMY® Awards, the CMAs, or the Academy Awards. Eat your heart out that you're not there, that you didn't win, or that you only won one. I think rewriting is overrated. If song X isn't working for you, write song Y, or rewrite song X; pirate parts of song X for song Y (heck, yes, you can't plagiarize from yourself); or keep song X around for laughs. But song X could inspire you to write song Y. Turn down my song, will you? Hah! (We'll show *them*, won't we?) Put down that Uzi. Pick up a pen. Write another song. Out of the ashes, the phoenix rises. Or write about that concept, the coming back to haunt the unbelievers. O, ye of little faith!

Let a disappointment and rejection fuel your creativity. The "I'll show them" factor has spurred many a creative moment. The numbers of writers and artists who came from schools or publishers or families who didn't appreciate them or who were downright dysfunctional is legion. But this doesn't have to be a sad comment on approval-seeking adults. This can be the way and the reason that wounds become gifts. These are spiritual gifs of sensitivity, empathy, self-expression, channeling, and transforming ugliness into beauty.

Let disgust fuel your creativity, too. "I can do better than that" has inspired many a creative effort. If you disagree with prevailing norms, customs, musical styles, attitudes, or the quality of somebody else's music, offer a tangible alternative.

— 438 —

"The Very Thought of You, My Dear" (Ray Noble)
Who turns your mind into jelly?

— 439 —

Swear a little, e.g., "Darn That Dream" (Jimmy Van Heusen and Edgar De Lange). How about "Dang Me" ("they oughta take a rope and hang me") by Roger Miller.

— 440 —

"What Are You Doing New Year's Eve?" (Frank Loesser). Good question. Make some promises or resolutions or plans and talk about them in your song, e.g., "I Swear" (Gary Baker and Frank Myers).

— 441 —

Tell 'em how you like 'em, e.g., "Any Man of Mine" (Faith Hill), "Do That to Me One More Time" (Toni Tennille).

— 442 —

Some jazz greats: Charlie Parker, Thelonious Monk, Charles Mingus, Louis Armstrong, Django Reinhardt (just reminding you). They each had characteristic improvisational styles that can be studied and imitated. Of course, you can't copy my E note, because I own that one, but you're welcome to the others. No, I think D7 is trademarked also.

— 443 —

Write an elegy.

— 444 —

Write a mystery play referring to dynamic Biblical duos: Adam and Eve, Essau and Jacob, Samson and Delilah, David and Goliath, Abraham and Isaac. Or what about the moment of revelation, the great conflict, etc. Perhaps another text, such as *Autobiography of a Yogi*, has something for you. Pick a creation myth, a Sufi story, a teaching koan, or a parable, and set it to music.

— 445 —

Scare yourself. Go bungee jumping. Go sky diving. Give a speech. Visit a rest home. Ask for a raise. Ask for an autograph. Call up your old teacher and thank him or her. In other words, if you're living at the edge of yourself, your creative chances are greater. So, go do something hard. An open mic? A poetry reading? A hair-raising movie? A marriage proposal? (Not recommended more than once.)

— 446 —

Restrict yourself. Don't use the tonic (one-chord) anywhere in the song.

— 447 —

Never go to the five-chord in the song (this is surprisingly hard).

— 448 —

Write out the shape of your melody on a piece of paper in dark ink. Turn the paper over and trace a melody that goes in the opposite direction. Then fold the paper over and do the same thing. Put your high notes where your low notes are, or put your high notes at a different place in the structure of the melody. (There's more about this technique in the appendix.)

— 449 —

Write a song about being in a hurry or having plenty of time.

— 450 —

What's easy? What's hard? About growing up, loving, leaving, getting over somebody or something?

— 451 —

This is an idea I heard from Pierce Pettis, who said he got it from John Stewart: Put your head between at least two and up to six loudspeakers broadcasting different types of music at once. Apparently this scrambles your music processing, so that you get a kind of juicy noise pool from which to write a new melody.

— 452 —

Go to a play. Go to an art gallery. Go to a museum.
A petting zoo? A paint store?

— 453 —

Study fortune cookies, cereal boxes, coupons, and other pieces of "found" poetry.

— 454 —

Picture your favorite relative and describe one of their quirks.
What? They don't have any? That's quirky.

— 455 —

What are your (forgivable) foibles? Your beloved belongings?

— 456 —

Consider the migrations of your ancestors. Why did they go? What
were they after? What did they find? "A people without history is like
wind on the buffalo grass" (Sioux proverb). How did your parents meet?
Grandparents? Are there any romantic family stories to preserve in
song? Stories of family heroism? Any black sheep in your family?

— 457 —

Pebbles and pearls.

"That Was a River" ("this is the ocean") (Susan Longacre and Richard Giles)
Compare the value of a relationship or what you know about love "now" with
what you knew "then."

— 458 —

Counterfeit a musical tradition. Write a sea chantey, a Childe ballad
recently discovered (penned by you, of course), or a shape note song.

Maybe the heyday of that music has passed, but maybe you could revive interest in it by adding to the tradition.

—— 459 ——

Wayne Carson once wrote a song that says, "We're alike as two snow-flakes." You expected him to say "peas in a pod" maybe? To me, there are three different levels of cleverness in lyric writing. Level one is where a pun is in the title. Level two is where a whole line of the song is used in the service of a pun. But level three, the quintessential level of skill, is where puns are imbedded in the song in such a way that you don't even register them. It's not just a play on words; it's playing with irony at a much deeper level. Wayne has a song like that. He talks about traveling through Snowflake, Arizona, and then way down in the middle of the second verse, he says he doesn't have a chance in hell of getting his woman back. You connect the dots yourself. See if you can aim for level three. You might get two, but you'll never get to three if you don't know it's there to aim for.

—— 460 ——

Get theatrical and fool around with your instrument. (That's probably why they call it "playing" music as opposed to "working" music.) If you play guitar, try damping down, pulling off, hammering on, using harmonics, or slapping the body of the guitar as part of your song. If God had intended us just to *strum* the guitar, guitars would be nothing but strings.

—— 461 ——

Here is the chord chart of a progression used by "Hound Dog" (Jerry Leiber and Mike Stoller); "Blue Suede Shoes" (Carl Perkins); "Jailhouse

Rock" (Leiber and Stoller); "Oh, Carol" (Howard Greenfield and Neil Sedaka); "Mabelline," "Sweet Little Sixteen," "Memphis, Tennessee," "Johnny B. Goode," "Roll Over, Beethoven," and "Rock and Roll Music" (all by Chuck Berry). (*Your song's name here.*)

1 1 1 1
4 4 1 1
5 4 1 1

— 462 —

George Brassens, the great French lyricist, made great use of one-noun titles. These can be very evocative, e.g., the Philistines, the gorilla, the orange, the wind, the bicycle, the garden, the gravedigger. Try wrapping your story around a single noun.

— 463 —

Celebrate music itself. "I've Got the Music in Me!" (Bias Boshell), ("there'll be") "Sad Songs (Say So Much)" ("to make you cry") (Bernie Taupin and Elton John), "I Write the Songs" (Bruce Johnston), "It's Still Rock and Roll to Me" (Billy Joel).

— 464 —

John Calvi played an icebreaker game at the Quaker Center one year with a group of us. Maybe his questions will spark something in you, too:

What is your secret addiction?
If you could have coffee with anybody, who would it be?

If you could travel around the world for a year with someone you didn't like, who would it be?

If you could send a message to world leaders, what would it be?

What's the worst thing you've heard in a meeting?

If you had one million dollars to spend by tomorrow, how would you spend it?

Tell something you've told no one else.

Name a new hotel.

What was your best or worst high school moment?

What was the best fun you ever had in a car?

Whose house guest would you like to be?

What's the best gift you could get?

What's your most unQuaker-like desire?

What's the worst insult you ever uttered in anger?

What's the biggest lie you ever told?

If you could steal one thing and keep it, what would it be?

— 465 —

Write a song about a hotel or motel, e.g., "Third-Rate Romance" (Howard Russell Smith), "Heartbreak Hotel" (Mae Axton, Elvis Presley, and Tommy Durden, "Hotel California" (Don Felder, Don Henley, and Glenn Frey). What about a restaurant, bar, waitress, e.g., "The Lady Who Carries the Tray" (Chuck McCabe), waiter, cook, pearl diver.

— 466 —

What would people see if you really did live in a glass house?

— 467 —

Hold yourself in your own arms. What is the kindest, gentlest, most merciful song you could make for yourself?

— 468 —

What cause would you champion in a song? For example, calls for ecology awareness were made in "Big Yellow Taxi" (Joni Mitchell), "Nature's Way" (Spirit), "Out in the Country" (Three Dog Night), and a rewrite of "Mercy, Mercy Me" originally by Marvin Gaye that Robert Palmer re-recorded.

— 469 —

Imagine you died yesterday. Write your own obituary. What accomplishments, relationships meant the most? Who would care most if you died? Comfort them.

— 470 —

Describe a wilderness.

— 471 —

Write a song about a secret initiation.

— 472 —

What did your parents never do? Are you a chip off the old block? Were you or should you have been adopted? Write a song for your dad or mother. If there are unresolved issues or your parents aren't around, you still have plenty to say, right?

— 473 —

When did you cease to be a child?

— 474 —

Write for your mentors and well-wishers. Who has enriched your life, cared, challenged, taught, and delighted in you?

— 475 —

Have you ever had any close calls?

— 476 —

Finish these phrases:

No matter how long I live _____.
No matter how hard you try _____.
No matter what anybody says _____.
How much more _____ will it take?

There's a heavy price to pay for _____.
It's so hard to _____.
It's so good to _____.
I always know when _____.

— 477 —

Should you or shouldn't you? Will you or won't you?
Stand at the crossroads and explore your options.

— 478 —

Write a song for group spirit, a revival, a communion, an offertory, a
"last supper" (or a first dinner on the ground).

— 479 —

Anticipate or suspend chords using a 4th above from one chord to
another, such as C7sus4 above C7 to resolve upward at F. Replace root
triads (1 3 5 chords) with sustained chords (1 4 5 chords).

— 480 —

Use some chord inversions. Put at least one chord extension (9ths,
11ths, 13ths chords) into your arrangement.

— 481 —

Try writing in a song form you haven't tried before. If you haven't written a song *without* a chorus, try that; or if you haven't written a song *with* a chorus, try that.

— 482 —

Write a melody that progresses in waves with each melodic shape higher than the last and each group of note values shorter than the last. In other words, speed up and lift your melody to hit a climax. Write a melody that soars.

— 483 —

Pretend you're Picasso. How would a Cubist tell your story? What are the facets and angular juxtapositions of ideas you could use? Put your eyeball on your shoulder.

— 484 —

Doesn't it feel good to be *alone* sometimes? Turn some assumed or accepted cliché on its head. For instance, alone doesn't have to be lonely. Or maybe there's no such thing as love at first sight; there's only love that is developed over time. Maybe you know some teenager who likes hanging out with his parents, or a really sweet mother-in-law, or a saintly (instead of wicked) stepmother. Or maybe you feel there is no honor among thieves, not all is fair in love and war, the weaker sex is the stronger, or nice guys finish first. Show how your life differs from the cliché.

— 485 —

Write on shelf paper, a grocery sack, extra-long legal pads. If you're right-handed, use your left hand to write. Write from the bottom of the page upward or from outward in. Use the margins. Sit in your chair backwards. Squat or lie on the floor. Draw your lyrics in the dirt with a stick or imagine them on the ceiling. Write tiny characters. Write big. Use crayons. Write in a spiral. Write in clusters. Draw cartoons to illustrate your lyrics.

Take up space . . .

S P A C E
P
A
C
E

— 486 —

Write a campfire song or a song for summer camp, as in this classic:

"Hello Mudduh, Hello Fadduh
(Here I am at Camp Granada
Camp is very entertaining
And they say we'll have some fun if it stops raining)"
—Allan Sherman and Louis F. Bush

— 487 —

I recently heard Utah Phillips say something truly empowering to a group of singer-songwriters: "Don't give 'em what they want to hear. Give 'em what *you* want them to hear."

— 488 —

Write a call-and-response song, where a line is sung and then answered by a group. These are community-based songs, especially prevalent in religious music and the African musical tradition. They're also powerful in establishing solidarity, forever.

— 489 —

Make faces while you sing. Play charades with your song title.

— 490 —

If you had a lost and found for dreams, what old dreams would show up in it?

— 491 —

Write a song before you're ready to.

— 492 —

Paint without a brush. Start a fire without matches.

— 493 —

When was the last time your teacher/preacher/pop icon acted human? How were they diminished in a moment of weakness or tenderness?

— 494 —

Spit it out. No, no, not your gum, silly! The truth you've been saving.

— 495 —

I got a huge kick out of writing a blues song with Betsy Jackson and Karen Taylor Good called "Brain Surgeon." One lyric went: "I'm a brain surgeon, baby; I want to play with your mind." How richly rewarding it was to later meet and play this for a friend of mine who happens to be—you guessed it—a brain surgeon! Think of a song that would be perfect for a particular person or occasion, and if possible, lay it on 'em. Yes, Richard Leigh wrote huge hits, including "Don't It Make My Brown Eyes Blue" and "Somewhere in My Broken Heart," but his most requested song? "The Night They Made the First Cub Scout," in honor of the Blue and Gold Awards Banquet. Go, Bobcats! Hooray, Webelos! You can make yourself useful or zot right into the heart of a person or a community with a song. Some friend of yours is having a tough time? A baby? A moral dilemma? Falling out of love? Falling in love? A crisis of faith: You can be right there with them.

— 496 —

Think of great collaborative relationships, e.g., Leiber and Stoller, Kelly and Steinberg, Mann and Weil, George and Ira Gershwin. Find out about them. Imagine imitating their styles and processes. Pretend you're working in a stormy, Gilbert and Sullivan relationship, where you both remain at arm's length. Collaborate via the mail, over the telephone, or at a prescribed time. At home. In a publisher' office. Try collaborating if you haven't. Divide up responsibilities or have a free-for-all dialogue. Respect each other and give each other's ideas some room. If possible, love each other and let your writing speak volumes on quality intimacy and friendship.

— 497 —

Clip pictures and articles about things you love and are working toward: vacations, new careers, children, etc. Or you can use souvenirs and photographs to help you remember your dreams and fond memories; these will become a part of your songs.

— 498 —

What are places you've always wanted to visit? Do something you never got to do as a kid. Ride a roller coaster. Stay up all night. Climb a tree. Jump on the bed. Mess up a pile of raked leaves. Have a food, water, shaving cream, whipped cream, or marshmallow fight in the kitchen. Invest in a whoopee cushion. (I got this idea from Doug Hall.)

— 499 —

Write a song about keeping silence, e.g., ("you say it best") "When You Say Nothing at All" (Don Schlitz and Paul Overstreet).

— 500 —

What the heck—get some sleep. Do some living. If you drop this writing / "self- expression" and do more listening, reading and quietly taking stuff in, you'll probably have a jillion ideas tomorrow. Sometimes you have to allow for the ebb as well as the flow. Let yourself have a fallow field so you can grow some beauties tomorrow. Don't call it writer's block. Call if writer's rest, or input versus output time, or making a living, or being a mom or dad, or doing something else that might take precedence. It's okay. It may be stupid, but you dare to be stupid, right?

Introduction to the
Second 500 Songwriting Ideas

I t's been about ten years since the first edition of this book came out. Has anything changed with respect to my songwriting? Yes and no. I've written and/or co-written another four thousand songs, put out eight CDs as an artist, gotten about 400 more cuts, and generally enjoyed writing full time; my kids grew up, I moved to Nashville, etc. But, no, songwriting is and will continue to be the activity it always has been for me: one that I love, that I believe to be transformative, and that I want to share the joy of. As my friend and co-writer Ellen Britton and I observed (in a song) recently: A candle is not extinguished by lighting another candle.

People who say that the music business is "competitive" are telling you a bunch of malarkey. The music business is as competitive or as cooperative as you are willing to see it and to make it. If you want to be befriended by and belong in a community of listeners, co-writers, lyricists, composers, arrangers, musicians, producers, engineers, songpluggers, etc., then you *will* be. A large percentage of the population is composed of music-lovers, like you, and that fact alone will be a basis on which to build friendly and cooperative relationships. I won't amend my previous edition's acknowledgements by adding names. This could go on for days with the enormous gratitude I feel toward so many who have helped with this book and have so enriched my songwriting life. Suffice it to say, insufficiently: that my gratitude is vast, heartfelt, and unending.

When I tell people that I write, on average, a song a day, most of them probably think it's weird to be so prolific. But let me tell you, I'm just adjusting your mental bar (and mine, too) upward, so that you get another benchmark for how easy this "flow of ideas" and creativity can be. Writer's block? Hah! Take THAT, you writer's block! We don't believe in you. Or as my friend Patti Mitchell said to me the other day, "There are no walls in your mind." I hope not, although there are lots of nooks and crannies.

Art is a confidence game—the flowering of confidence in yourself, in your uniqueness, in your validity, and in your point of view. Some people call thought "the Akashic record," i.e., the idea that there's an over-arching, permanent and infinite fund of consciousness, of culture, of memory, and of imagination that we all may tap into. Songs and song ideas are like raindrops. They're falling all around equally outdoors, but only some of us rush outside with our arms out-stretched and our faces lifted and our tongues hanging out, ready to "catch" them.

Only some of us believe that these blessings—these creative little rain-drops—are meant for us. They're out there, in plenty, for all of us. So working on your self-esteem to consider yourself available and worthy of these gifts is as important as any song craft, or as important as any writing or composing tech-nique that anybody can divulge. I can only point out the abundance. The way I do that is by scoffing at perfectionism and, as before, by sharing some creativity exercises. These aren't necessarily titles or my ideas. These aren't songwriting ideas so much as they are some ways to *get* ideas, of your own, with your name on them. Personally, I'd rather have my songs be of such service that whoever wrote them wouldn't matter. For instance, with "Happy Birthday to You," I forget the originators but I can't forget the song. I love and use that song every birthday. Get ego out of the way and let the song in. Pass along the gift. Allow yourself to be of service. We don't get to keep any of this.

Guy Clark told me a wonderful story about Townes Van Zandt. Townes said, "I've most always been crazy. I remember the day it started. I was in fourth grade and my teacher held up an orange and a grapefruit. 'Now, class,' she said, 'this is the earth and this is the sun. The sun is a fiery ball, burning up. In about one hundred million years, the sun's burning out.'" Townes waved his hand frantically from the back of the room. "What is it, Townes?" the teacher asked indulgently. Townes stood up with his hands on his hips, red-faced, in great consternation, his voice thick with betrayal. He said, "Do you mean to tell me that the sun's BURNING OUT? Do you mean to tell me that I'm supposed to get up and brush my teeth and comb my hair and shine my shoes and show up at school every morning and the SUN'S BURNING OUT?" Guy said that, ever after, when someone—an authority figure, a concert promoter, a traffic cop, a record label executive, a preacher, a teacher, someone throwing their weight around—would lean on him, Townes would say, "Excuse me, but are you hip? The sun's burning out!"

I love that story. It makes me laugh so hard. I could tell it a million times and never get over how perfect it is. Many people, especially songwriters or people who are in the entertainment business, question themselves. Is what I'm doing valid? Important? My answer is, yes. Yes, of course. It's as meaningful or meaningless *before* you found out that it (and you) won't be around forever, as it was *after*. You give whatever you experience all the meaning it has. Songwriting is as justifiable and rewarding as it ever was, for its own sake. Not even the greatest song on earth will be around touching people forever; not if the only person the song touches deeply is you, the writer of it or if the song is played and sung to millions of people, nor even if it lasts for generations. The truth is that the people your song matters to won't remember it forever. So if immortality is your motivation, get over it. The sun's burning out. Now that we've got that little bit of egotism out of the way, we can relax and enjoy the small, un-ambitious, frivolous, imperfect—yeah, stupid—stuff we do. Songwriting, it's just fun, and you don't need to get it right, just get it down. Dare to be stupid.

In addition to five hundred more "songwriting ideas" or ways into the generative process that I'm scattering throughout this book, let me expand on a couple more writing techniques and issues that I've happened upon in another (twenty or more) songwriting workshops I've given for NSAI and Belmont University, Club Passim, Fishtrap, CCMC, SFFMC, Camp Harmony, and others.

A-number one, the songwriting aesthetic: What is it? How can you tell a "good" song? A good song has integrity. This can be understood cross-culturally, without regard to personal or idiosyncratic preferences. I mean integrity in two senses: in a thematic sense, as in sincerity, and in a structural sense, as in hanging together as one thing. Integrity is the main songwriting aesthetic or ideal to strive for, in my opinion.

We can't tell if you're telling THE truth but we can tell if you're telling YOUR truth. There will be congruence between your gestures and your intentions. If I hold my fist up and say, "Come here, I want to hug you," you'll run the other way. You sense a conflict between my gesture and my intention. Similarly, if your music and words fit each other, if the story and the emotion you're conveying is conveyed together, we (the listeners) will know. It's an absolute and unmistakable experience when someone's gestures and intentions are in consonance with each other. Even if we disagree or don't care for the way a person's feeing or point of view is being expressed, we all know when someone is being true to himself or to herself. We get it. That's how lie detectors work. There's no affect, no pulse-accelerating physiology of recognition when a lie is told. We are palpably moved in the presence of our own and another's truth. And there's beauty, a seamless flowing, in great melody and harmony of expectations tendered and met. The rising and falling action of tension and release, of motivation and payoff, of verse and chorus, is part of what songwriting is about. A series of promises are kept.

Just as in a joke, there is relief in following a song to its conclusion, because not only do we often encounter something surprising which releases tension, but our worries are unfounded. The first joke ever told is "Peek-a-boo," in which a baby is first worried that Mama or Papa are gone away for good, and then relieved when they reappear. The baby has no sense of object permanence, so covering a baby's face for a moment is tantamount to scaring him or her that they've lost their adult playmate. What causes laughter is the baby's reassurance. Happy reassurance, i.e., that the connectivity of a melodic line that this note, this section, this meaning, is following another, is part of what makes great songs great. They move from one part to another with the natural ebb and flow of tension and release, of balance and contrast. Anyway, that's my theory of humor and song-form in a nutshell. The parts of a song are intended to set up and play off each other. Adhering to formal constraints is yet another way to squeeze creativity like a tube of toothpaste out of an activity, giving rise to the ecstasies of play. One of my favorite authors, Soren Kierkegaard, describes a kid in school playing with a beetle and a walnut shell on his desk. The small theatre of his accomplishments, the narrowness of his constraints, is paradoxically *why* the boy is able to be such an artist. In choosing yes, I like potatoes and no, I don't like tomatoes, the existentialist (and artist) is declaring his or her identity. Art is about choicefulness—the smaller, more exacting the arena, the better.

(By the way, if you want to limit the scope of your topics, I recommend writing chiefly love songs because, as Harlan Howard said, "What do people *most* care about?") We promote and promulgate what we focus on, talk about, sing about, read about, write about, think about. If you're expressing anger in your songs, or co-dependence, you might want to slow down and take a look at what you're communicating. Songs are more like sending letters to others than just getting things off your chest. There's a terminus to your writing. Even if it's an imaginary audience, there's a listener. You'd never spit on someone; I urge you not to do the musical equivalent.

My favorite quote about songwriting comes from my co-writer, Tom Kimmel, when he was asked to be a judge at the Kerrville "New Folk" songwriting contest. He came out to give the obligatory speech before handing out prizes, and said, "People will tell you that this is not about the performance; it's about the songwriting. But I'm here to tell you that it's not about the songwriting, either. It's about what the songs are *about*." In other words, the motives and values which songs point to *outside* of themselves and their impact on the people who listen to them—yes, *that* matters.

Okay, so now we have an aesthetic (integrity), which is some way to "evaluate" the completion and merit of a song. Other books might tell you more about this and/or apply additional aesthetics, give you checklists and editorial rubrics and norms. I'm deliberately not doing that in this book because, as I said before, I'm constitutionally against the idea of algorithm-like or recipe-like songwriting. I believe that critique is hard on the generative process. In some ways, to be a writer or an artist of any kind, one needs to bifurcate his or her personality. On the one side of you is the playful, childlike, generative self, and on the other side is the editorial, self-aware and critical self which checks and perfects your work. Both "selves" are needed to write a song, but not talking to you all at once! Send the latter (the editor/the judge) out of the room when the former (the creator) wants to try out his or her ideas. If you split your writing process or your personality into these two parts, and give your creative side free rein at first, you can go back and re-writer later. More ideas with power, more awful, more wild and exciting and unworkable ideas will be generated. But hey, they're compost! To grow some prize roses, you need a little compost. Originality is a good thing. In order to move forward with your writing, it's a good idea to tell your finisher, your polisher, to take a hike while the raw materials are being explored. This book is about foraging for song seeds. Be lavish and wide-ranging. Die Gedanken sind frei (the mind is free). It's not that "anything goes." It's that anything goes *at first*. Make a practice of not worrying about much beyond authenticity. Do I contradict myself by talking about game playing with little rules and restrictions? So be it. Choosing what will not be included is a creative activity too. Silence is your friend.

I believe that your maximal creative output, i.e., what you enjoy and achieve in the way of diving into the process of songwriting and further, what will enable you to "flow" with it to its completion, will be helped by focus. *Focus*, not on the details, not on the mechanics, not on the judgments and opinions of yourself and others, but on *what* you're saying, *what* you're doing, *what* you're communicating. If you have a song with everything but integrity, you won't really have a song. And if you have a song with a lot of integrity, its flaws will be subsumed under the emotional experience of it. The little restrictions you place on yourself that have to do with form, time signature, range, coherence, singability, economy, aesthetics associated with logic, poetry, storytelling, universality, sensory detail, and so on, are fine. I recommend that anybody engaged in songwriting, study and apply additional aesthetics to write "better" songs. But the one absolute aesthetic—the one that counts, in my opinion—is integrity. Even that one needs to be put on hiatus while you're starting the engine, cranking up the old furnace. It's really okay to just begin. This "idea book" is to help you find your own ways into the song, to give you more creative sparks. It seems to me that worrying about whether your song is good, "real," commercially viable, a hit, or any other evaluation you want to make of it, will just get in the way of the flow of your ideas.

What I said before about fear being the gatekeeper to the floodgates of inspiration is still true. And judgments are, unfortunately, more fear-based than self-expression is. Therefore, I recommend that you initially count all your little glimmers of ideas equally, uncritically. You can then go back and do your weeding out afterward. Is this line still in 4/4 time? Is this what a Cajun lady really would say in a song about the bayou? Given that a Cajun lady in the swamp is my character or the song protagonist of choice, well, do I have consistency in her speech patterns, in her musical gestures? Could I locate my song within a stylistic tradition, a compelling "voice," and do I really want to say (through her as an alter ego) whatever this song is saying? Who is the singer? Who is the one sung about? Who is the singee (the one sung to)? And, what are they singing for?

Talking about song protagonists brings me to my other main, newfound creativity exercise. I learned this one from Tom Paxton. You don't have to write about yourself. I'll repeat this because it's such good news. You don't have to write about yourself! In other words, that adage, "write what you know" is limited. You can write what you *imagine*! The trick is learning to empathize. I've given the following as a co-writing exercise on more than one occasion. First, I ask people in a group to pair themselves. Then I ask each partner to tell the other a story about themselves, something that happened to them, something that they learned from. I ask people to figure out a point to their story, ask how it made them feel, and I encourage them to get details from their partner. Storytelling takes about five minutes per person. Then I ask people to reverse roles so that each person has a story heard. Then I ask people (selected victims) to tell the larger group their partner's story in first person, as if it happened to them. Then, with a little tweaking, a short form described and a "title" culled from summing up the stories, we're off and running into writing "each other's" songs from "each other's" stories. Walking a mile in somebody else's moccasins is one of the most powerful ways I know of to write and to co-write. A whole world opens up to you for songwriting. There are stories and points of view under the surface of your nearby friends and neighbors that you never guessed. You can cast your consciousness to Alpha Centauri, for that matter. Talk about eye-opening! I have witnessed amazing sharing and understanding of each other's experiences as stories unfold: students who were former soldiers on opposite sides sat next to each other; a man sat next to a pregnant woman; a woman sat next to her son. Fundamentally, the group's emotional tone lifts because we generally like each other when we know each other better. If you have to tell someone else's story, you quickly find out what it is you missed, or you don't get, or feel the same or differently about.

Does this exercise lead to songs with integrity as well? Yes, because what you explore is the human condition, and the more you can resonate with others, the more you can write sensitively and honestly, and even better, co-write. What we want to know is: does my song sound like a human wrote it, or did a Martian or a robot write it? Check. Do an Integrity 101 check.

Case in point: People called up the radio stations playing the hit song "Who I Am," sung by Jessica Andrews. The chorus lyric starts: "I am Rosemary's granddaughter; the spitting image of my father, and when the day is done, my mom is still my biggest fan." The song goes on as a young woman is declaring triumphantly, honestly "And that's *who I am*."

Jessica Andrews was seventeen and her fans were teenage girls, calling up, practically sobbing to the deejays about how wonderful the song was, how it touched them, how it was about them. She was singing their stories, how could she know them so well? It was much like the feedback Lori Lieberman and Roberta Flack reported when they sang "Killing Me Softly" (Norman Gimble and Charley Fox) "He was singing my *life* with his words." How could the artist know them so well? How could Jessica have captured who they were, how they felt? And yet, Jessica didn't write that song. It was written by Brett James and Troy Verges, two men in Nashville in their 30's and 40's. Empathy, folks! Empathy: the ability to (or the attempt to) see the world the way someone else does.

So here are my two longer songwriting ideas. (They are longer than fits into the grab bag of ideas that the rest of this book is intended to be.) Number one, the big Kahuna is: Hold integrity as an aesthetic, but leave any judgments or aesthetics (trying to improve your song) in abeyance until *after* you get it going. Two, try empathy as a stance from which to write. Integrity and empathy will automatically move people, and then you won't have to worry about your song being "popular." People like to be moved.

As a music publisher Liz Rose was heard to remark: "We are in the business of buying and selling emotional experiences." Or perhaps in less marketplace-oriented terms, that is to say, songs function as emotional levers, as catalysts, for the emotions we carry around with us. It's a beautiful thing to remind ourselves of our own emotions and of our shared humanity. Songwriting is a great big, juicy, emotionally (not to mention spiritually and intellectually) challenging and absorbing pastime. So let's get to it. What have we here? One thousand ways to launch into a song, to get us to "feel" like writing. Ah, Archimedes: "Give me a lever and a place to stand and I will move the world."

Speaking of moving the world, here's another one of my favorite songwriting-related quotes. Chairman Mao Tse Tung said, "If you wish to lead a people, be their poet." Songs have incredible power to change us and to change the world. "Amazing Grace" was written by a former slave trader who quit doing what he was doing after writing that song: "I was blind, but now I see." Or as my blind friend, Ross Winetsky, ever-mindful of discrimination against people with disabilities says, "Why couldn't they just say he was stupid and he made a mistake?" Sure, let's say it and play it and sing it and write it until we "right" it. That's yet one more songwriting idea, a freebie. We'll call that 1001 . . . "Try leading a people."

Daunting as it may be, even though you have, as Harlan Howard put it, "a tiger by the tail," it doesn't mean you get to be intimidated by your own power. Yes, songs can be important and powerful. Yes, they're potentially world-changing and life-changing. Songs could get you fame and fortune and sex; have you "win friends and influence people," as Dale Carnegie says; make you laugh so hard that you cry, and cry so hard that you hiccup. Songs can heal the worst pain of all, the feeling of loneliness, of abandonment, of separation. Songs reconnect us to each other. Somebody's in the same boat. Somebody hears us, feels the same way, knows what it's like to be us. And our human potential is shown to us by great songs. Aren't you glad and proud to be a member of the same human race that produced Beethoven? I sure am. As my friend John Knowles said, "Music is like a mountain. The closer you get to it, the bigger it is." But just because music is this huge thing that you could spend more than a lifetime on and never "learn" or "finish" or "get to the top of," or "get to the bottom of," doesn't mean that your songwriting has to be this serious, difficult enterprise to prove to somebody-anybody-everybody that you're great, that you're really something special. You already are. So take the heat off and have fun. And don't forget to goof it up on the way, with gusto, and don't care.

Why? So that we can really get down to the creative nitty-gritty. So that patterns will emerge from chaos. So that we're standing around priming the pump when a gully washer hits us. So that we can be in the way of grace when Heaven decides to hand us a song. *That* kind of not caring. You mean we might be doing something dumb, like waiting around for things that haven't happened yet, for risking disapproval, for creating songs that might never lead to ever being heard, to anything, we might be—gasp!—wasting our time writing songs? Yep. That's what I mean.

That's the key to creativity, I think. Disengaging process from outcome maximizes creativity. Or as Lorraine Hansberry put it in a play she wrote: "What use are flowers?" That question is what creative people like us, everywhere, answer every day of our lives. Paradoxically, part of beauty's usefulness is its uselessness.

The Second 500 Songwriting Ideas

— 501 —

Re-title the paintings in a museum.

— 502 —

Dramatize wildness, exotica, wilderness, and obstreperousness, e.g., "Wild Things" (Chris Williamson), "She's a Wild One" (Jaime Kyle, Pat Bunch, and Will Rambeaux). *Where the Wild Things Are* by Maurice Sendak could give you ideas.

— 503 —

Two cellmates in a jail, bunkmates on a ship, or cabin mates at boot camp talk about what they'll do when they get out. If you were free/freer/done/out from under somebody's thumb, what would it be like?

— 504 —

Tell us how to enjoy spring. What do you see in a garden? Use horticulture as a metaphor for life lessons. Peter Sellers did that in the movie *Being There*, and people made him president for it.

— 505 —

If you overheard somebody's confession or you had one of your own to make, how would it make you feel? Ashamed? Glad to get it out? In answer, would you be furious, sad, benevolent, forgiving? Songs about forgiveness are very powerful. One of my favorites is "The Randall Knife" by Guy Clark.

— 506 —

What's so surprisingly sad about a wedding? What's funny or inspiring about a funeral? What's the unexpected thing?

— 507 —

Put the fun back in dysfunctional. Use a family get-together as a backdrop to a lyric. "Merry Christmas to the Family" (Robert Earl Keene Jr.)

— 508 —

Do Be Wah Da . . .

Scat, using vocal improvisation (as opposed to instrumental improvisation) to get new melodic material. First, use eight beats, over a simple pentatonic scale (CDEGA); then scat over longer periods. (The more melodic material you cover, the more your techniques will change.) Hearing Louis Armstrong and Ella Fitzgerald, the masters of scat singing, will blow your mind—guaranteed. New York Voices or The Swingle Singers are good role models too. Also, vocalese, improvising new lyrics to pre-existing songs, e.g., John Hendricks and Eddy Jefferson in Lambert, Hendricks, and Ross.

—— 509 ——

Use three colors to describe the sky, and moods that do the same.

—— 510 ——

Write an ostinato (a repeating melodic part) such as a guitar riff or a bass line that doesn't match your primary melody. Record the rest of the melody over it on a different track.

—— 511 ——

Write a song about dressing for a date. "I Enjoy Being a Girl" from *Flower Drum Song* (Rodgers & Hammerstein), and "I Feel Pretty" from *West Side Story* (Bernstein), are songs from musicals that have girls preening and planning to go out. Stephanie Davis and Don Schlitz wrote one that Garth Brooks had a hit with, about a man who is dreading his date, "Learning to Live Again is Killing Me." Bobby Pinson and I wrote "I Wish Your Block Was the One I'd been Around."

—— 512 ——

Write two songs you could sing simultaneously with a partner. This isn't a round or a duet per se, but two separate lyrics that could go together, e.g., "Rock My Soul" and "He's Got the Whole World in His Hands." At one time, my twin sister, Erika and I learned lots of these. ("Partners," "I Found a Horse Shoe," and "Mangwanempulele" were some of our folk favorites.) Madrigal rounds often used different lyrics that fit together in each of the melodic sections. For instance, "Hey, Ho Nobody Home," "Soul Cake," "Rose," "Ah, Poor Bird," and "God

Rest Ye Merry Gentlemen," all fit together. Trust me; this is fun as well as challenging. Another great example of this sort of thing is found in Meredith Willson's *The Music Man*: "Pick a Little, Talk a Little," "Goodnight My Someone," "Seventy-Six Trombones."

— 513 —

What's something surprising that you found in a pocket? For example, Michael McNevin's "Second Hand Stories."

— 514 —

Finish these:

What I always wanted most was _____.
It wasn't hunger for food, it was hunger for _____.

— 515 —

Have a regular place—a corner in your home or office, or the studio, or the park—that is your writing space. It's Pavlovian. You might stimulate the writing activity by seating yourself in a location that has been habitually linked to writing. (Ring any bells, anyone?)

— 516 —

If you could undo one experience of your life, or if you could do over, or extend one, what would it be? Re-live one day of your life, or one experience. Be your mom or dad, doing the same thing in their life.

Or pick three days in your life together, to show their impact, e.g., "Three Days in a Row" by Dave Berg.

— 517 —

You give some change to a homeless person. You recognize them or they look up and say, "I know you!" Who are they, and how do they know you? You get a ride in a taxi, get served in a bar, or see somebody's name in lights, e.g., Harry Chapin's "Taxi."

— 518 —

"And then I go and spoil it all by saying something stupid . . ." (Carson Parks, sung by Frank and Nancy Sinatra). What always happens when you fall in love? "What Do You Get . . ." (Burt Bacharach and Harold Arlen) "Here You Come Again" (Dolly Parton)

— 519 —

There's no such thing as telling a story too many times. Point of view makes all the difference, e.g., *Grendel* by John Gardner or *The True Story of the Three Little Pigs* by A. Wolf (told by Jon Scieszka).

— 520 —

Experiment with different writing tools. Don't use paper at all. Go directly to tape or CD. Make edits audibly. Use a palm pilot stylus; write without an instrument; with or without pencil, pen or computer. Try using different combinations of tools.

— 521 —

What is something that you or somebody else thought was no big deal at the time, only to find out that it was a really big deal later? (Jana Stanfield) "If I Had Only Known"

— 522 —

Write a song about an unfair punishment that you endured or something unfair happening to someone else. What outrages you? What still rankles? What did you learn?

Could you let it go?

— 523 —

Have you ever had a conversation where no one is saying what they really mean? Marilyn and Alan Bergmann once wrote a whole libretto in which the dialogue (spoken) was at odds with the actual thoughts (sung). Great idea for an operetta or a funny movie, I thought, let's have more of this. The film *What Women Want* covered some of that topic.

— 524 —

Create a portrait of a person, five characteristics you think of with respect to that person. What explains their prominence? What makes this or that characteristic stand out? Analyzing artists and their previous work is a good way to start "target" writing. What do they sing about, mostly? What do they leave out in the songs they sing?

— 525 —

Here are some sample topics: Moving, traveling, having to change my life again, what I want my life to add up to, twists of fate, ethical dilemmas, things I have saved, outgrowing childhood labels, the stories about our births, our re-births, traditions, rebellions, a letter to a future you, my favorite gifts then and now. How have your ideas changed? Where were you when . . . (e.g., when John Lennon died, when the twin towers were hit?)

— 526 —

Take a random paragraph from a book or a book title and write a new first or last sentence to bracket that paragraph or line. Or, pull out half of a line or a word from the middle of a book or title to get a line or a title for your song. Dictionary hopping can be entertaining also.

— 527 —

Something about the situation seemed "off." What was it?

— 528 —

Give advice. Explain to a man how best to attract a woman. Explain to a woman how best to attract a man. Explain how best to keep love going, e.g., "Back at One" (Brian McKnight), "Treat Her Like a Lady" (Lionel Ritchie), "That's the Way Love Goes" (Janet Jackson, James Harris III, and Terry Lewis).

— 529 —

Write music appropriate for worship in a tiny chapel, a grand cathedral, an outdoor setting.

— 530 —

You're sorting through clothes of someone absent. You're sifting through a cigar box, a drawer, a closet, a jewel box, a piano bench, a garage. What did somebody leave behind that's revelatory?

— 531 —

That worst date/the best date you ever had. The blindest.

— 532 —

Finish these phrases for titles:

The _____ at the end of the journey.
_____ cities.
Bright as _____.
The _____ memory of him or her.
Holding tightly to his _____.

— 533 —

Put some nouns (or nuns) together in a song, then adjectives. Mix and match them. For example, bus, smoke, sidewalk, stars, magazine, telephone, soprano, subway, harbor, bread mixed with green, honey, hopeful, open, rare.

— 534 —

What is the perfect lunch/picnic/dinner/breakfast for lovers? What are people eating in songs, anyway? "Crawfish pie, filet gumbo . . ." (Hank Williams). Rick Beresford has a great song called "Chicken Fried" and the late great Dave von Ronk sang about "One Meat Ball." "Frim Fram Sauce" (Nat Cole), "Save the Bones for Henry Jones" (Nat Cole with Johnny Mercer), "Push-Ka-Pee-Shee-Pie" (Louis Jordan), "Everybody Eats When They Come to my House" (Cab Calloway).

— 535 —

There are two typical methods of writing: (1) vowel sounds leading to making sense, i.e., melody to lyric (Paul McCartney's, Billy Joel's, Beth Nielsen Chapman's and John Hiatt's method) and (2) structure, story or plan leading to making sounds, i.e. lyric to melody (Gary Nicholson's and Steve Seskin's method). Try the other method for a change, or write with somebody who does it your way.

— 536 —

Banner days! The rainy day, summer vacation, flying,
a family reunion, the first day of summer.

— 537 —

Choose a room with a view to write "from." Sketch a scene—the bar
stool, the high apartment window, the mountaintop, the cage, e.g.,
"Pacing the Cage" by Bruce Cockburn.

— 538 —

What makes person "X" tick?

— 539 —

Write a postcard in your mind. Pick a place to write home about.

Finish: I've never seen anything that looked like this _____.
There are so many _____. The quality of _____is amazing.

Or, write a letter from a place you've never been.

— 540 —

"The Song Remembers When" (Hugh Prestwood)
As the credits roll in your memory file, what's playing?

— 541 —

Tell about the first night with the puppy, kitten, or the birth of a calf.
Getting up early to fish, hunt, or photograph animals.

— 542 —

What as the first gift you ever gave, how and why?
What was the best gift you ever gave, how and why?

— 543 —

Console someone who just got rejected by their high school sweetheart,
or got bad news from their school principal, mechanic, doctor,
banker, lawyer, or neighbor.

— 544 —

Describe your own version of "Lake Wobegon" (Garrison Keillor) or a
Norman Rockwell painting. There must be some quiet, bucolic, maybe
bygone, small town that you could wax nostalgic about, i.e. "Little
Bitty" (Tom T. Hall), "Memphis in June" (Paul Frances Webster and
Hoagy Carmichael), "Atcheson, Topeka and the Santa Fe" (Johnny
Mercer and Harry Warren), "Folks that Live on the Hill" (Peggy Lee),
"Dayton Ohio, 1903" and "Dixie Flyer" (Randy Newman).

— 545 —

Compare happiness to an animal, or to an animal's happiness.

— 546 —

Nick Dobson and Karl Coryat recommend doing one of these as a way to take the heat off (expel your inner critic):

(a) Write twenty songs in one day. Built in is the assumption that they won't be perfect. You didn't have time, right?

(b) Set fire to the paper after thirty minutes after you've copied a few lines.

(c) Find some stylistic or aesthetic distinctions you normally try to hold or balance and break them: dissonance versus consonance, beauty versus ugliness, humor and seriousness. Mix it up. Find the boundaries or definitions and cross them.

— 547 —

Someone in your family says: "There was something I always wanted from you and that was _____." Someone in your family says, "It's time to tell you something."
What does he/she say next?

— 548 —

Start song ideas with these phrases:

The fragile _____of hope
_____as Tarzan
_____children
_____Christmas
Hot as _____
Back _____
Calm as _____
True as _____
_____as New Orleans
As likely as a trip to _____

— 549 —

Who did an old lady with seven cats, some spinster sisters, the post-man, a man with a fishing pole down at the dock, the lighthouse keeper, the doorman, the crossing guard, used to be?

— 550 —

Have a dialogue with a person or a thing in your dream.

— 551 —

Go to a writers retreat, a writing conference, a song camp, an instrumental workshop, a writers group, or hold one. Leave your workaday responsibilities behind for some immersion in the task.

— 552 —

Pick a flower, a shell, a rock, a household object; pick another person, a child, a celebrity. Tell what you see in them. What would someone else see?

— 553 —

The cornucopia, the bottomless well, seven league boots, the magic mirror, the aspirin, the panacea, the answer to pain or the answer to deprivation; what do we all need, and why? "Love, Sweet Love"? Hal David and Burt Bacharach were onto a good thing.

— 554 —

Read the newspaper and get a song idea from a story. Or, take a head-line and make up a story without reading the article that goes with it. Woody Guthrie, Lenny Bruce, and Mort Sahl each wrote songs and bogus articles inspired by the newspaper of the day.

— 555 —

Walk through a shopping mall. Use a listening station at a store. Put your satellite radio on the widest possible genre-mixing search.

— 556 —

What if Cinderella never went to the ball? What if Beethoven had never gone deaf?

What if Tom Sawyer lived in New York?
Change history, or change fictional history.

— 557 —

Concentrate on a stranger. Guess where they live, their occupation, personality, habits, marital status, and their history. What are your clues? Finish: In the lines of his/her face, I saw _____.

— 558 —

What is something funny, something eerie, something hard to understand? What can you make simpler and more accessible from your own experience by singing it?

— 559 —

Put a story in the mouth of one of the people in it.
Write the ending to a story.
Create a plot backwards.

— 560 —

Cut out pieces of an existing melody. Find a point at which it's unrecognizable. Mark Simos calls this "Reader's Digest" tune-smithing.

"Out in the West Texas town of El Paso . . . one little kiss and Felina, goodbye."
(Marty Robbins, borrowing from himself)

— 561 —

I heard it said once that animals are people without power. Who else is without power? How can they get some?

— 562 —

Reverse engineer some similes, e.g., Love is like a baseball . . . how?

Love is like: Venus, a waterfall, a vampire, skiing, a mushroom, snow, chocolate, the blues, a rope of sand, a foggy day, a cactus garden, an elevator shaft.

— 563 —

Harvest stories of Southern hometowns. William Faulkner, Carson McCullers, Sherwood Anderson, Thomas Wolf, and Gregory McDonald have all given songwriters a wealth of imagery to draw on.

(See Mac MacAnally, Bob McDill.) "Birmingham" (Randy Newman), "New Orleans" (Hoagy Carmichael)

— 564 —

Habits.
What are yours?

Pick an experience that you have every day of the week such as evening prayers, sitting down to breakfast, dog walking. Free associate about that experience afterwards every day for a week.

— 565 —

Letter writing: Part two.

Have you left some important things unsaid with a relative or friend? Do you have another writer or artist to thank? Maybe you could write a song tribute to someone who passed away recently. The likes of . . . will never be seen again.

— 566 —

Ask questions from unlikely viewpoints such as: What do ants think about? What does the man in the moon see? Why does the pot call the kettle black?

— 567 —

What musical distraction do people in dentists' offices, traffic jams, etc. need to help them get through the experience?

— 568 —

Systematically mix or pair people and their surroundings. Use a map to get there or make up destinations, e.g., Lois Lane—Daily Planet, Adams family—mausoleum, Dr. Spock—Starship Enterprise, policeman—patrol car. Put familiar people in unfamiliar settings, or get them to travel from one place to another.

Ever been to Sopchoppy, Florida? (Tom T. Hall)
"He Broke My Heart in Three Places" ("Seattle, Chicago and New York, Toledo, Minneapolis, St. Paul, Miami, Chattanooga, Montreal.") (Milton Drake, Al Hoffman, Jerry Livingston)

— 569 —

What would you see if you were invisible, or were a fly on the wall?

— 570 —

What did you once love about summer, winter, spring, or fall?

"I'll Remember April" (Don Raye, Gene DePaul, and Patricia Johnston), "September Song" (M. Anderson and K. Weill)

— 571 —

Describe a walk on a winter night. Imagine peering into windows.

What's going on in those houses, those stores?

— 572 —

How did you play house as a child?

Was it war, dolls, school, hospital, castaways?

— 573 —

What is your ideal man/woman?

— 574 —

What is a grandiose idea that you had as a child? What were some totally inaccurate ideas you had as a child? What disabused you of your most fanciful notions?

What did you keep on believing?

— 575 —

Describe a man's thoughts buying lingerie, or flowers, or jewelry, or candy.

— 576 —

Compare two objects that are similar. Maybe one is fake and the other is real, or one is smaller than the other like a dog, a stuffed animal; a lemon, a plastic lemon; a watch, a clock. Make comparisons about relationships too. For example, Steve Gillette's "She's Not You" or "Why Can't He Be You" (Hank Cochran, recorded by Patsy Cline).

— 577 —

Thanksgiving—the holiday, the feeling.

Write a song about what you have to be thankful for. Billy Smith and I did that one year in a song called "What I'm Thankful For." I was gratified to learn that the Sunday after Thanksgiving he sang our brand new song in his church. My friend Joe Vinikow says it's not a musical holiday. Too much tryptophan toxemia.

— 578 —

Write a biography of your co-writer or make up a speech to introduce them, and swap. This exercise may spark a song idea or help you get to know your co-writer better, appreciate them more, and incorporate your stories into songs. You can leave out the ex-spouses. Only they can write about them . . .

— 579 —

Swap alternating lines or verses and choruses with your co-writer.

Do a division of labor differently this once. Tom Kimmel and I wrote a song whose first four lines were lyrically and melodically his and whose second four lines were lyrically and melodically mine, but no one could ever tell that the verse was divided in that way. The process and the outcome of your co-write can be you and your co-writer's secret, if it's cohesive enough.

— 580 —

What's extraordinary about an ordinary day?

"Feelin' Groovy" (Paul Simon), "Pleasant Valley Sunday" (Gerry Goffin and Carole King), "Sunday Morning Coming Down" (Kris Kristofferson)

— 581 —

A man is not crying, but you know his heart is breaking. How do you know?

— 582 —

A young couple is moving into a house where an old
widower is moving out.

What does he tell them?

— 583 —

A farmer who is losing his small farm is speaking to the auctioneer.

What does say?

— 584 —

What's the value of your old friends? Tell them in a song.

— 585 —

Oh, the bittersweet job of parenting, the mixed results of
matchmaking. When you tried to control an outcome, how did it go?
Show how a good idea can backfire.

— 586 —

We not only hear sound, we feel it. Songs are written *from* and *to*, or
are intended to impact different areas of the body—chakras. There are
head, heart, pelvis, and feet songs. They move, usually, from higher to

lower frequencies. Try writing a song to affect each of these areas, or light each one up like a pinball machine—er, videogame.

— 587 —

Choose a photo from a magazine or a family album, a painting, or a drawing. Make a character in the picture tell the story of why they are in that position or where they are going. Have them leave the painting or photo. George Seurat's painting was the inspiration for *Sunday in the Park with George* by Stephen Sondheim.

— 588 —

What place does artistic freedom have in your life?

"Paint the Sky Green" by Julie Rust, "Tell That to Michelangelo" by Georgia Middleman and Steve Seskin, and "(I'm going to make a great big noise with my) Little Voice" by Sally Barris

— 589 —

You are on an airplane.

Imagine singing to or having your seatmate sing to you. What is his or her song?

— 590 —

Make a big deal out of little actions like baiting a fish hook, opening a bottle of champagne, pulling out of a parking space. Method acting is about gestures and so is descriptive songwriting, to some degree. "I Say a Little Prayer for You" (Burt Bacharach and Hal David)

— 591 —

What's so good about homemade things? Chris Crawford and I wrote a song called "Home Made Fire." It was a double entendre about his chili sauce.

— 592 —

What do we have time for?

"The List" is a wonderful song about this by Tim James and Rand Bishop.

— 593 —

"D-I-V-O-R-C-E" (Bobby Braddock and Curly Putnam) sung by Tammy Wynette. Consider what divorce does to kids, marriage myths, a song in defense of the old-fashioned institution, or in defense of making changes. "I'm Movin' On" (D. Vincent Williams and Phillips White). How do you move on? George Strait declared it in "All My Exes Live in Texas" (Whitey and Lynda Shaffer).

— 594 —

Everything about the way she/he looked could be summed up in one word.

What was that word? There's your next song title!

— 595 —

What did you think you could never forgive, that you forgave?

When you are face-to-face with God, what do you say?

— 596 —

How did you know it was love? "Beware!" (Louis Jordan)

— 597 —

There's something you see *in a different light*—morning sun, dusk, lamplight. What does a different light have to do with how you feel?

Determined. Restless. Moved. Passionate.
How do you feel these in your body?

— 598 —

How does passion make you behave? What is passion worth? Write about the last great love scene you saw/loved/imagined.

— 599 —

Ah Ha! Vision: Part Two.

You are looking at the surface, then beyond that, then beyond that. Looking not only at, but looking into something or someone. See the expression, the skeletal, the bones under the face, the hidden emotions, the motives.

— 600 —

Some writers work with sampling keyboards. Sounds and timbres will inspire a tune. Compose a little theme music to show off each sample in your keyboard's library. Do the same thing with each rhythm.

— 601 —

Try using augmented chords to replace 5^7 e.g., E7 → A can be used in place of 4 → 1 in the key of A, especially in soul robato intros like "You Don't Miss Your Water."

— 602 —

Some instruments lend themselves especially well to some harmonies and not to others. For instance, the dobro is particularly appropriate for songs in G tunings. My friend and co-writer Todd Cerney recently remarked that fiddling vocalists were able to create more interesting "weaving" harmonies around the melodic line than people who sang regular bluegrass harmonies, because mandolin and fiddle players exclude the middle, making vocal use of the 1 and 5 more than the thirds. Both mandolin and fiddle players use double stops frequently, most always thirds, but the vocals go someplace else.

— 603 —

With a partner, play copycat with a flute, xylophone, harmonica, or guitar. Select a few notes and have your partner play them back. Then have your partner make a change in a note or note value (duration), then another, then three, etc. The object is to teach (or stump) your partner and to gradually build a shared melody. You can evaluate a melody in tiny increments, keeping what you like as you go.

— 604 —

Strike a surface with a spoon, mallet, or drum stick. Play talking drums by echoing your first pattern or patterns to create a "musical conversation."

— 605 —

Make a little opera out of a day. Sing everything to your kid. "How are you this morning? Would you like some milk with your cereal? Now we're putting on our socks."

— 606 —

Syncopate familiar tunes. Push the beat on one or two of a four-count phrase, or put the accent on the second or third beat in a march instead of firsts and thirds. Cheryl Wheeler created a wonderful song called

"Potato" to the tune of the "Mexican Hat Dance." The songs "We'll Go Honkytonkin'" (Hank Williams) and "I Am an Orphan Girl" (Gillian Welch) both move a beat forward in the fourth line of the last stanza to create syncopation. Cool idea. Try it, you'll like it. Look at almost anything by Jimmie Rodgers, "Honky Tonk Man" (Lefty Frizzell), "Here Comes the Sun" (John Lennon and Paul McCartney).

— 607 —

When you make a little change after a lot of repetition, you make a big impact. Repetition creates tension; afterward there's release. For instance, in the words of The Beatles, "You never give me your money, you only give me your funny papers," staying with one note gives the last note's rise in pitch more drama. If you set up a lot of rhymes and then don't rhyme once, the same sort of effect occurs. It's like "Where's Waldo?"

The little thing that's different is exciting.

— 608 —

Try walking a bass line that strays from the notes in the chord. In the key of C, the bass can go step-wise: C to B to A, to G to F. And some of those steps will provide a lot of harmonic movement. "This Kiss" (Beth Nielsen Chapman and Annie Roboff) has an ascending bass line, while "Mr. Bojangles" (Jerry Jeff Walker) has a descending bass line. See also "Cannon in D" (Pachelbel) and "Friend of the Devil" (Robert Hunter and Jerry Garcia). Go up in the bass when the melody goes down and vice versa; don't go where the melody goes with the bass.

—— 609 ——

Wax extroverted, where the end of the verse really lifts, such as in an anthem or praise song. Contrast, writing something with lots of low notes—an intimate, almost whispered melody. In "Freebird," Lynyrd Skynyrd goes from a ballad to a jam.

—— 610 ——

This is an idea from Kenn Boostrom having to do with your co-writer or associates. Basically, his model has to do with hiring people in a brainstorming or company context, but the same could apply to co-writing. The idea is to connect with some unlikely pairings. It is generally known, as in dating, which people will get along well, will be fun, and easy to co-write with. They are people who are complementary and compatible. But consider, if you want innovation—something fresh—in your writing, you might be well-served by a slow learner, a thickheaded writer or listener, Joe Man-on-the-Street who needs to have stuff spelled out for him (or her). Maybe they don't get your obscure lyrics or abstract poetry. Maybe that's just what you need to keep your work simple and focused. If you need to translate and paraphrase things, they sometimes get clearer.

Look at somebody you dislike or are sure their ideas, values or background are so different from yours that you'll really stretch yourself to hear them out.

Be sure to hear them out.

A novice, somebody new to the biz, can keep you from being stale and can lead to surprising pitching prospects.

Encourage dissent at the editing level, not at the idea-generating level. Tussle. Work for and defend your ideas with someone who plays devil's advocate.

— 611 —

Drive. Take a road trip. Sing to yourself. Carol McComb has a theory about why this works so well. She thinks that if you are doing a repetitive or boring activity, only part of your attention is at liberty. This creates a "drone" analogous to a bagpipe or some other stable core of music that forces inventiveness in the higher registers above it. By partially entraining your mind, the rest roams freer. Weed whacking, or doing the dishes are some other good pre-songwriting activities.

— 612 —

Use the approach of "Orinoco Flow" (Roma Ryan and Enya), which has an Arabic flavor, or "Smooth" (Rob Thomas and Itaal Shur, performed by Santana and Rob Thomas), with its Latin flavor, to create hybrids of American and world music. Try songs that are half in one language and half in another. They catch a lot of ears.

— 613 —

It turns out that kids have an easier time skipping over a lift and descending diatonically through than ascending diatonically through it. Also, it's easier for kids to sing skips in intervals, especially descending skips, than to sing straight stepwise patterns. This is some of what's known about kids' ranges and tessitura, if you are writing kids' songs: Grades K–1, D^4 to B^4, grades 2–3, E^4 to E^5, grades 4–6, B^3 to E^5, where the superscript is a piano octave.

— 614 —

Contrary to popular opinion, songs are rarely about one emotion. The juiciest are often written when you have mixed emotions. In your journal or notes, whenever you experience mixed emotions, make a note of it. That's an especially-fertile field for deep song harvesting.

— 615 —

Soren Kierkegaard, one of my favorite authors, said, "Life may only be understood backwards, but it must be lived forwards." You know more about life than you think you do, and we want to hear your wisdom. Here are some line openers:

What makes you think I'd _____ ?
Now that _____
It's hard to understand _____
You _____ me
I _____ you
_____ ty and _____ ty
_____ in' and _____ in'
_____ ly and _____ ly
_____, of course
How could you _____ ?
_____, Baby.
Baby, _____
That's _____ now
Wait _____
Right _____
_____ for all my life.
What are you gonna do about _____ ?
If I start _____

— 616 —

Grow up/ act your age/ settle down

What were/are your reactions to these admonitions?

— 617 —

What rings your chimes? Finish these phrases:

My mission in life is _____.
Our mission in our relationship is _____.
My calling is _____.
The area I want to do selfless service in is _____.
I have an urge to explore _____.
I've always wanted to be _____.
Lately I've thought of trying _____.
_____ would be a great adventure
What I want to share with the world is _____.
I think I have a gift for _____.

— 618 —

Lorraine Hansbury tartly exclaimed, "If Adam had talked to Eve, she wouldn'a' had to visit with the snake!" What are your opinions about the communication habits of the opposite sex? "This is me you're not talkin' to" (Randy Travis), "You Talk Too Much" (George Thorogood), or "Talk to Me" (Sam Cooke).

— 619 —

Why use ordinary ink? Why not write in blood? (Just kidding.)

Conflict, violence, and the history of an eye for an eye such as with the Hatfields and the McCoys, the Crips and the Bloods, Tutsis and Hutus. Oh, yeah, have I mentioned Arabs and Israelis, Indians and Pakistani?

— 620 —

If life is a relay race, what is your torch or baton?
What do you most want to convey to the next people to come along?

— 621 —

Write a song about a boat that went down, e.g.,

"The Rueben James" (Woody Guthrie)
"The Wreck of the Edmund Fitzgerald" (Gordon Lightfoot)
"The Jeannie C and The Mary Ellen" Carter (Stan Rogers)

— 622 —

People frequently tease the ones they adore, and everyone knows that eight-year-olds usually change their minds about the initially-icky opposite sex, e.g., "Don't Take the Girl" (Larry Johnson and Craig Matthew Martin, performed by Tim McGraw). Write about the early stages of a relationship. My lifelong friend Roger Edwards and I had an amazing antipathy in junior high. Who knew that, cued from our hateful beginnings, we were destined to be together for over forty years?

— 623 —

Progress
Have you made any?

— 624 —

Show an alien or a blind date around town and write about it.

— 625 —

"Time marches on." What else marches on? Do you feel like commenting on army ants, cockroaches, boll weevils, locusts?

— 626 —

Write a song that features furniture or fixtures: sofa, couch, bed, table, porch lights. There are so many great ones out there. My favorite is Janis Ian's "Jesse." Also, "Every Light in the House is On" (Kent Robbins), "We Just Couldn't Say Goodbye" (Boswell Sisters).

— 627 —

Write about carrying a torch for someone.

— 628 —

Drive without the radio on.

True story: Dave Brubeck allows no radios anywhere in his presence.

— 629 —

Have you ever heard of a genre of music called filksongs to accompany science fiction stories? No? Do you play them on the theremindolin? Illustrate a science fiction or a fantasy in song. One of my favorite writers in this genre is Kathy Mar.

— 630 —

A reversal of hook placement is a fun thing to try. John Braheny has cooked up a list of places to put hooks in a song that I think you'd get a lot of creative mileage out of trying. They are: Repeat the same line two or more times; first and third lines of lyric the same, second and fourth lines different; first and third lines the same, second and fourth lines the same; first three lines the same, the fourth are different, all four lines different; the first or last part of each line is repeated; the first and last line the same, the second and third are each different. In other words, when you're thinking about what part of your song to repeat and how to use rhyme and meter to deliver a pattern, you might as well exercise your options and try all the different ways. The game's afoot.

— 631 —

While Jack Saunders and Shake Russell celebrate Texas cooking and landscape, Emily Kaitz introduces a food, "Pico de Gallo." Have you told your mama lately how much you appreciate her cookin'? "Red Beans Cookin'" (Marcia Ball)

Lindy Hearne and I wrote a blues called, "Soup's On" ("you don't know what you've been missin' 'til you've messed around my kitchen.")

— 632 —

Hawaiian, e.g., Van Rozay, Bob Brozman, George Kahumoku, Ledward Kaapana. George said that Hawaiians often start by musing on the natural beauty around them and make use of environmental sounds, incorporating them into their music. We should all be so lucky to have our surroundings sound so beautiful.

— 633 —

Frank Herbert's eulogy to his wife, Heinlen's eulogy for Theodore Sturgeon. . . I'm telling you, people, there is some of the most inspiring and moving writing out there to give you ideas for what you want to say when it really matters to you. When you wish you had something to give your loved one, including and especially when you miss them in their absence, write them a song.

— 634 —

Write about the death of a child.

— 635 —

Finish:
I'm _____and this is my story.
I'm _____and this is my swan song.

— 636 —

Stand up for what you believe in, in a song.

— 637 —

Why should she/he love me?

— 638 —

Use all three kinds of seventh chords in the same tune. In a harmonized scale, the 2, 3, 5, and 6 chords may all be dominant 7ths.

— 639 —

Stick a movie idol in your song, especially a romantic duo. There are some doozies out there to choose from. Remember Bogie and Bacall? Hepburn and Tracy? *Sleepless in Seattle*? These are also potential song titles.

—— 640 ——

Lament somebody's stuffiness. What has become of
their former joie d' vivre?

"Where Did the Wild Horses Run To?" by Melissa Javors.

—— 641 ——

Celebrate weaving, quilting, sewing. These are very different in industrial
versus community or family contexts. Carla Sciaky's "Weaver's Song"
collection or "Threads" by Joni Bishop.

—— 642 ——

Somebody's prickly. Write a porcupine song. Wayne Henderson
and Bill White did that, and there's "Cactus Tree" by Joni Mitchell,
and that line in John Hiatt's song, "Thing Called Love" ("I ain't no
porcupine, take off your kid gloves.")

—— 643 ——

Try writing ragtime. That style typically proceeds around the circle
of 5ths, in dominant 7ths. An example of a ragtime progression (1, 6^7,
2^7, 5^7) is "Rag Mama" by Blind Boy Fuller. "Sweet Georgia Brown" and
"Salty Dog" are other examples. Ragtime (most popular at the end of
the 19th century before the 1920's) was a syncopation of melody against
a steadily-accented accompaniment. Write a song for Scott Joplin to
have played on his piano-player rolls.

"Take Me to the Pilot" (Elton John and Bernie Taupin) and "Signed, Sealed, Delivered I'm Yours" (Stevie Wonder/Garrett, Wright, and Hardaway) are examples of modern ragtime. See what classic rag is doing chordally, then apply that same progression to a more current, peppy 4/4 song in a call/response form.

— 644 —

In stride piano, the left hand "strides" the keys aggressively while the right hand plays a melody. Fats Waller, Jelly Roll Morton, Art Tatum, and Willie the Lion Smith gave us some strides to live up to. Uh, down to. Uh, back and forth to. And don't forget the greatest of them all: James P. Johnson, author of "Charleston," "Old Fashioned Love," and "Carolina Shout."

— 645 —

Try "tone clusters." These are dissonant chords of adjacent notes or a-tonal music (without reference to key) as written by Roland Kirk, Cecil Taylor, Charlie Mingus (or Edward Toth, Shostakovich, etc. in the classical vein).

— 646 —

Let's have some reggae, irie, Mon. Blend it into something with just a hint of reggae, with the off-beats strongly accented. Jimmy Cliff and Bob Marley rock, but Seal's a great exemplar of that subtle hint of reggae in modern pop.

— 647 —

Write some progressive jazz using "portamento." Slide from one note to another without articulating notes like Stan Kenton and Charlie Parker.

— 648 —

Samba began in the movies in the 1930s with Carmen Miranda. The first record registered as a samba was in 1916 in Brazil, but we could pile some bananas or mangoes on somebody else's head, now couldn't we? Bossa nova means *new wrinkle or new wave.*

Let's put a new wrinkle in the rhythm.

— 649 —

Write a Habanera-style tune or Cu-Bop a la Machio and Mario Bauza. Try the precursor of sambas, the choro.

— 650 —

Some people say the most natural way to start writing a song on the guitar is to play a G chord and sing a B note, or, in C, singing an E. Well, we're going to monkey around (or as Will Smith says, "get jiggy with it"), but might as well do it the easy way.

— 651 —

The chorus to "Santa Claus is Coming to Town" is a great example of a principle Steve Dorff and Dick Goodwin once taught me whereby you set up a pattern by repeating yourself a couple of times and then break it, just once. You can do great stuff by moving a note forward or back in the phrase, changing the rhyme scheme, elongating or shortening the duration of the note, giving a surprise note out of the initial key that is expected to stay in, or going in a different direction (up versus down in pitch, big versus little interval steps). There are lots of ways to fake us out, but like dribbling in basketball and misdirecting your guard so you can pass behind, you must first get going in some direction.

— 652 —

Lamont Dozier said the song "Stop in the Name of Love" didn't originally stop in the melody until they recorded it. This is a funny story and an object lesson in letting the prosody (how the words fit the music) dictate what you do next.

Have you used a stop in your melody lately? Does your lyric tell you to do something and are you paying attention to her? "How Sweet It Is To Be Loved by You" (Holland, Dozzier, Holland)

— 653 —

Robert Bly's writing exercise for a men's group: Pick an object. Write five minutes of description, no allegory. Then take a break. Have five more minutes of writing, answering Bly's question, "How does this object relate to your father's shame?"

— 654 —

How do you give yourself a hard time?

— 655 —

The historian Thomas Carlyle said that if you "see deep enough . . . you will see musically; the heart of nature being everywhere musical if you can only reach it." Pythagoras thought so too—that the very fiber of the universe was music and mathematics. To him, they were one and the same. I know I've mentioned this as a writing technique before, but it's so neat, I want to emphasize it. Find some mathematical or natural pattern, and see if you can describe or echo it with music. What do beautiful mathematical patterns, such as putting intervals to constants such as *e* or *i* or *pi* or the *Golden mean* sound like? What elegant structure can you imitate or initiate in music? Maybe you could come up with a new one. Wouldn't that be something!

— 656 —

Scales. The scales fell from my eyes. Some other types of scales:

Major (Ionian) 1 2 3 ♭4 5 6 ♭7 (Or, in steps: whole, whole, half, whole, whole, whole, half.)

Natural Minor (Aeolian) 1 2 ♭3 4 5 ♭6 ♭7 (whole, half, whole, whole, half, whole, whole.)

Harmonic Minor 1 2 ♭3 4 5 ♭6 7 (whole, half, whole, whole, half, whole, whole.)

Melodic Minor 1 2 ♭3 4 5 6 7 (whole, half, whole, whole, whole, whole, half.)

The Natural Minor starts on the sixth of the major scale.

The Harmonic Minor is the same as the Natural Minor except the seventh note is raised a half step.

The Melodic Minor is the same as the Natural Minor except the sixth and seventh notes are raised by a half step.

Ionian ♯5: 1 2 3 4 ♯5 6 7

Dorian 1 2 ♭3 4 5 6 ♭7

Phrygian 1 ♭2 ♭3 4 5 ♭6 ♭7

Lydian 1 2 3 ♯4 5 6 7

Mixolydian, 1 2 3 4 5 6 ♭7

Pentatonic 1 2 3 4 5

Neapolitan (half, whole, whole, whole, whole, half, one and one half, half.)

Hungarian (one and one half, half, whole, half, whole, half, whole.).

Hungarian Minor (whole, half, one and one half, half, half, one and one half, half.)

Chromatic (All the notes in an octave, including the sharps and flats.)

Blues Scale 1 ♭3 4 ♭5 ♭7
Country Blues Scale 1 2 ♭3 3 5 6

Start a song with a stepwise progression of notes; simply go up or down a scale. Get a theory book and try using each one of the scales in a walking stepwise melody. Take a staff note and select a playing range of each scale. Define a high note as the starting point and a low note as the end note of your playing range and reverse it. Look back and transpose first—possibly an octave. A MIDI keyboard works great for this.

— 657 —

Fernando Sor is considered the Mozart of the guitar. His etudes are unparalleled. He wrote them to work out different fingers. One piece was especially to exercise the ring finger. Try writing for one part of the hand or another, or one technique of playing, such as flat-picking versus pattern finger picking (Travis style versus Chet Atkins style, e.g., boom-chuck with the thumb versus chuck-boom, boom-chucka, boom-chucka).

— 658 —

You are enfolded, cherished, and loved.
Imagine that!

— 659 —

Check out Lorraine Hansberry: "Me Tink Me Hear Sounds in De Night" or Langston Hughes "Mulatto." Write about slavery and oppression. Mark Aaron James said in a lyric of his that "Everybody's got an Egypt." Yes, everybody's got some place or something to escape. And everybody's got his or her own Exodus and exile, too.

— 660 —

We've all been through the gauntlet:

Growing up
Acting our age
Settling down
What others will think
Taunts
Disability, ostracism
Ridicule, "Don't Laugh at Me" (Allen Shamblin and Steve Seskin)
Even responding to pressure to put together a heterosexual nuclear family can be a drag (pun intended) and a good song.
"When Will I be Loved?" (Phil Everly)

— 661 —

How do you talk yourself out of the blues?

— 662 —

Take "Twinkle Twinkle Little Star" and put the accents on the second and third instead of the first and third beats. Try syncopating other familiar tunes.

Sing "Take Me Out to the Ballgame" in 3/4 time. Now try jazzing it up in 4/4 time. Unexpect the expected.

— 663 —

Make up a kid's song using getting ready for school, going to bed, killing your sister or brother (just checking to see if you were paying attention), or mealtimes as a theme.

— 664 —

Wear thimbles or Band-Aids on all fingers or put buttons in the tops of thin gloves or mittens. Scratch and tap out rhythms on a tabletop. Paradiddle steering wheel, dashboard, anyone?

— 665 —

Play inside/out, near/far, loud/soft acoustic guessing games.

— 666 —

See if you can hear your eyelids blink, your heartbeat, your breathing.

— 667 —

Aldous Huxley said, "The perusal of a page from even the most beautifully written cookbook is no substitute for the eating of dinner." How this applies to songwriting is to listen to somebody else's music, not passively, but as if you could follow it back to the place it was written from. Be there with the writer, meditatively sharing their physical space, then go "taste and see" for yourself.

— 668 —

The five parts of Grofe's Grand Canyon Suite are:

Sunrise
Painted Desert
On the Trail
Sunset
Cloudburst
Now, write your own desert or canyon "suite."

— 669 —

"The future is not what it used to be" (Mickey Newbury). Neither are we.
"My Get Up and Go Has Got Up and Went" (Pete Seeger)

Write a song a cynic, a misanthrope, a hypochondriac, or a curmudgeon would be proud of if he weren't feeling so poorly. He's "All Used Up" (Utah Phillips).

— 670 —

No one told you it was black tie.

— 671 —

It was the weather's fault.

— 672 —

The hospital bed had been designed for someone much larger.

— 673 —

It was off limits when you were young.

— 674 —

The tackiness was what you liked about the place.

— 675 —

The place hadn't changed, but you had.
(The lockers and the desks are really small at your old grade school.)

— 676 —

What hasn't been said about Peoria? Paris? The Wall?

— 677 —

He said/she said. Here are some starters:

He said he would help me.
She said I could do anything.

He said I was young.
She said I had no sense of adventure.
She said I got what I deserved.
He said "They're not like us."

— 678 —

Write songs for demented and convalescing people or use depressing ideas
for the terminally happy, e.g., that tree won't grow/that dog won't hunt.

— 679 —

Write your "mission statement"—your purpose in life.

— 680 —

Go to a sensory deprivation tank,
or take an amusement park ride in which you
hang by your heels and spin, or
use Ganzfeld (white noise in your ears and half ping pong ball
cups over your eyes). Get some radical shifts in your consciousness
and put yourself in The Zone.

— 681 —

Pass around a piece of paper and play "telephone" where each person
adds a line to make a group co-written song.

— 682 —

With a pentatonic (5-note scale) write descending melodies like:

"Goodbye to Innocence" by Madonna and Shep Pettibone, "Listen to the rhythm of the falling rain" (John Claude Gummoe of The Cascades, recorded by Ricky Nelson), Sam Cooke's "Don't know much about the Middle Ages" in "What a Wonderful World," Donovan's "First there is a mountain, then there is no mountain," and Crosby, Stills, Nash & Young's "Where are you going now, my love?"

— 683 —

Write some scales of ascending modulations as in "Tea for Two"
(Vincent Youmans and Irving Ceasar)

Modulate up 2 whole steps
Key C → E
Dm7 → Gm7 → Cmaj7 → Fmaj7, staying on the E note
A beautiful example of this is the line, "Ain't got a barrel of money," in "Side by Side" (Harry McGregor Woods)

— 684 —

Pick a key that's especially suited to one instrument or another. For instance B♭ is a horn-friendly key. Dobro is especially appropriate for G tunings. Do the obvious arrangements, but then also do the obscure, adventuresome ones. What sounds are *atypical* of that style or band configuration?

— 685 —

Imply 6/8 over a cha cha. Tap one 123, 123 on one hand and 1 2, 1 2 with the other hand. Try your hand at Peruvian rhythms: festejo (12/8) or zamacueca (6/8) or combine them, as Oscar Stagnero does in "Festejo para Tere," Where the bridge is played accenting beats two and three and then goes back to festejo but it feels like the zamacueca triplets.

— 686 —

Timbre. Some writers work with sampling keyboards just to play with sound quality.

Try composing theme music for each sound patch.

— 687 —

Songs with two chords:

"Come to my Window" (Melissa Etheridge)
"Here you go . . ." in "Crystal Vision" (Stevie Nicks)
Sheryl Crow's "Strong Enough (to be my man)" major → minor
"How Would I Know" (Melissa Etheridge)
"Jambalaya" (Hank Williams)
You see? It can be done simply.

— 688 —

Go minor → major → minor → major

Examples are: "867-5309" (written by Alex Call and recorded by Tommy Tutone) or "The Power of Love" (Gunther Mende, C. DeRouge, J. Rush and M.S. Applegate) or The Backstreet Boys' "I Want it That Way" (Max Martin and Andreas Carlsson): F# min → D → A → F# min → D → A → F# min → D → A → F# min → E → A

"I Concentrate on You" (Cole Porter)

"Steppin' Out with my Baby" (Irving Berlin)

— 689 —

Use what Gary Talley in his video, *Guitar Playing for Songwriters*, calls "connecting chords." If the key is F, for instance, and the progression is F → A → C or 1 → 3 → 5, you could "connect" F to A with F# or F/A. For example: 1/3 where 3 is the base note in a root chord, or 5/7 where 7 is the base note in a dominant chord, are "connecting chords." When moving 1 → 4, the first inversion tonic chord is a passing chord, e.g., C → C/E → F.

You can do the same with the 5 chord in the first inversion, with the third interval of the chord in the base voicing. 1 → 1/3 → 4   C → C/E → F

4 → 1/3 → 2m   F → C/E → Dm

1 → 5/7—6, 5/7 → 1

Or in G key: 5 → 5/7

D → D/F#

Or G → F# → Em

Or G connecting to Em

Or cycle through dominant 7th chords along the circle of fifths as in "Salty Dog Rag" (Red Foley)

G → E7 → A7 → D7 → G

G → B7 → E7 → A7 → D7 → G

The common progression 4 → 5 sets up a mood in the intro and 5⁷ will tell you what key.

— 690 —

Lift one finger in C position and move it back and forth to give
C → Csus4 → Cadd9 (and you can do the same with Gadd9, etc.).
Preserving chord shapes on the guitar is a great way to generate melodies.

"Your Love Amazes Me" (Amanda Hunt-Taylor and Chuck Jones)

— 691 —

A thorn by any other name would prick as much. Name that thorn.

— 692 —

Phil Spector got a groove called the baion from the Brazilian film
soundtrack, "Anna." He fell in love with it and many of The Drifters'
hits, including "Save the Last Dance for Me," "Spanish Harlem,"
"Stand by Me," and Barry Mann and Cynthia Weil's opening for
"You've Lost that Loving Feeling," all use that groove.

Hint: if it was useful before, it might be again.

— 693 —

The Beatles used a Balkan rhythm: 123, 123, 12, 12 in "Here Comes the
Sun" and nobody thought twice about it. Amazing what you can get
away with in modern pop using World Beat rhythms!

— 694 —

What do "Gentle on my Mind" (John Hartford) and
"El Paso" (Marty Robbins) have in common?
No chorus!

How about "The Reason" (Mike Trainor) and
"Long Road Home" (Steve Earle)?
No rhymes!
You could remove something most people would think is essential to song structure and see if, in fact, it really is essential.

— 695 —

Women and religion, tequila and handguns.
What causes trouble?

— 696 —

Cumbias, boleros, merengues, charangas, pachangas, rumbas, cuecas, sambas, son y danzon. There are lots of Latin options out there/in there. Adelante y atrás.

— 697 —

How do you stay affirmed, renewed, energized, enthusiastic and inspired about what you do? Remember the highs.

— 698 —

Take an existing song and write a parody. Then write
a new melody to the parody.

— 699 —

The Orkney guitar tuning, I learned from Steve Baughman, is CFGGFC
and sounds like "dropped D" or DADGAD (except more like dropped C)
tuning with its ringing open G giving Orkney a harp-like quality.

— 700 —

Have you ever written in a foreign language that you know?
That you fake?

— 701 —

Try to top yourself.

You *know* you can better your last song or at least do a respectable sequel.

— 702 —

Try "Taro patch" tuning—the most common slack key guitar tuning.

— 703 —

Joe Vinikow told me that skiers have a saying, "Go big or go home."
When you're traveling forty miles per hour on less than one inch of
fiberglass separating you and all kinds of terrain, you don't take time to
consider each bump and curve. Sing a song for the big picture. What do
you want to sing to a huge, rowdy crowd? What will get and keep their
attention, expand their minds and hearts like helium balloons? What's
the biggest, most impacting chorus melody you can write?

— 704 —

There are certain professions that seem to be particularly helpful to songwriters. Lots of songwriters are also carpenters (constructing songs; handy
with wood; sometimes luthiers, repairing and making their own instruments), realtors (doing speculative work before actually closing), waiters
and waitresses (jobs you can find in most locations to work around flexible
schedules and entertainment establishments), teachers (the summer–off
types), and counselors. Go figure. Put some day-gig skills into your writing.

— 705 —

Orchestrate for Doctor Doom.
Pipe music into his laboratory, his castle, his videogame.

— 706 —

I know at least three people who have written entire albums of baseball songs.
Pick a sport and some people to honor. Chuck Brodsky had a song adopted
by the Baseball Hall of Fame. The obvious place they need sports anthems is

the Olympics. Ray Bonneville and I wrote a song called "The Greatest Party of Them All." But what about a theme song for the March of Dimes, the Special Olympics, and other organizations that sponsor great physical efforts?

— 707 —

Can you un-ring a bell? Un-say something? Do you wish you could, or do you wish somebody else could?

"Un-Break my Heart" (LA Babyface Edwards)

— 708 —

"May the Bird of Paradise Fly up Your Nose" (Neal Merritt, recorded by Little Jimmy Dickens) Hmm. Is that a blessing or a curse? "May you live in interesting times." Ah so! Obviously a curse. How about writing a song to bless us or curse us? If you're sufficiently inventive, you might confuse us as to which is which.

— 709 —

Tell or write a whole story, and pick eight lines to keep. Or, take a synopsis of a story or a film treatment, and transfer it to lyrics. What does your story boil down to?

— 710 —

Joni Bishop and I came up with a bumper sticker for Nashville's spiritual community. See if this makes writing easier: "Bad Songs Happen to Good People."

— 711 —

Everybody's doing something. You aren't. What is it? You're out of school, out of line, out of step, out of sync, out of sorts, out of turn, or maybe just out.

— 712 —

Un-requested love.

— 713 —

Introductions before singing a song are most commonly lots of 5-chord or vamping between the 1 and 5, or 6-, 2-, 5, or the end of the song for eight bars repeated, or the end of the song for four bars repeated, or some other snippet of the song (such as the turn-around) repeated.

Here's an idea. Why don't you imagine yourself in some club before the band is going to launch into your tune? Play the introduction for yourself then launch into your composition. What Lewis Carroll said about relating a story was, "Begin at the beginning." If you get yourself on the runway and meditate on what it feels like before singing a cover tune, then maybe you can write one for somebody else. (Ironically, to do this, you're beginning at the end.) LA vocalist and teacher Jeanne Pisano once advised people to introduce a song by talking about some aspect of its premise without identifying its title before you perform it. The old strip tease approach—it works.

— 714 —

The Sierra Club had an article on developing a relationship to the place where you live. For example, knowing what the local average rainfall is might not go directly into your lyrics, but paying close attention to your surroundings might. Likewise, your answers to self-test questionnaires or relationship questionnaires in the back of women's magazines might not find their way into your lyrics, but then again, they might.

— 715 —

Go from flat 5 to 4 some place in your progression, and see what that does for you. Anybody for a 1 chord with a 3 in the bass? DEElicious!

— 716 —

Use chord substitutions to re-harmonize more richly, e.g., $1 \rightarrow 4 \rightarrow 5$ becomes $1^{+9} \rightarrow$ sus4 $\rightarrow 5^{+9}$

— 717 —

Use the relative minor with the second two beats of a four-beat phrase.

Example:
G $\rightarrow$ Em $\rightarrow$ Em9 $\rightarrow$ C $\rightarrow$ Am $\rightarrow$ Am9 $\rightarrow$ D. Substitutions and extensions, G is equivalent to Gmaj6, Gmaj7, Gmaj9, etc.

— 718 —

Use your software to cut and paste. Move melodic motifs and song sections around in whole pieces like a jigsaw puzzle.

— 719 —

Talk somebody out of a bad mood.

— 720 —

Commiserate.

— 721 —

Write about criminal activity sympathetically. For instance, "Lady from Baltimore" (Tim Hardin) takes the part of a thief. "Jerusalem Tomorrow" (David Olney) takes the part of a con man. Bruce Springsteen has a song about a policeman whose brother has run afoul of the law, and don't you just love "With Catlike Tread" in *Pirates of Penzance* (Gilbert and Sullivan), "Miss Otis Regrets" (Cole Porter), "A Policeman's Lot" (Gilbert and Sullivan), and the big one, "Mack the Knife" (Kurt Weil)

— 722 —

Fan the flames.

— 723 —

Nah, douse the flames—who needs another fire.

— 724 —

Travelers. The homeless.

— 725 —

Make Biblical places allegories for where you are headed or what you are going through. "By the Waters of Babylon" (William Dillard); "Walkin' in Jerusalem Just like John" (trad.); and "Christ, You Know it Ain't Easy" (John Lennon and Paul McCartney)

— 726 —

If you're finding it difficult to reach somebody, tell them in a song, e.g., "Broken Bicycles" (Tom Waits).

— 727 —

Write something in 12/8 time. Exaggerate the triplet strum if you play it on guitar as in "Earth Angel" (Jesse Dalton, Gaynel Hodge and Curtis Edward Williams) or "Blueberry Hill" (Fats Domino).

— 728 —

David Mamet recommends omitting the third and concentrating on the missing tone. For example, in the key of C, en route, C to G, we hear the E anyway. In literature, Chekhov, Ionesco, and Pirandello de-emphasize the plot in their drama. Pinter removes the history, the narration; Beckett removes the characterization. We don't miss these features in their art. We give our listeners similar credit to elaborate, to estimate, to predict, and to enjoy surprises. Joe Vinikow adds: "The idiomatic effect of omitting the third is to create harmonic ambiguity—is it major or minor? This is appropriate for modal accompaniment (Celtic, Old Timey). Open fifths also produce a stark, powerful sound as in Shape Note or Sacred Harp singing. Thirds are also omitted in "Power Chord" heavy metal or grunge guitar accompaniment, as the open fifths are clearer in lower registers at high volume. Classical harmonists have traditionally avoided open fifths as harsh and primitive sounding. In jazz harmony, the fifth is the sacrificial interval as it is harmonically redundant, i.e., it has no bearing on whether the chord is major or minor, or whether the 7th is major or dominant." Thanks, Joe, for another bee for our bonnets and more grist for our mills.

— 729 —

Play rhythm changes a la "I've Got Rhythm" by George and Ira Gershwin, and write a new melody on top. Successful examples of this are "Doodlin'" by Horace Silver and "Lester Leaps In" by Lester Young. The verse is: Gm → Cm → Gm → E♭7 → Gm → D7 → Gm → D7 and the chorus is B♭6 → Gm7 → Cm7 → F7 → B♭7 → B♭7/D → E♭7 → E°7 → B♭6 → / F → F7 → B♭6 → F.

— 730 —

"Ignorance with confidence!" reads the sign on a friend's banjo case.

Not just a motto, a way of life. This reminds me of another friend's lead-guitar teaching technique. If you, while you were jamming in his group played a mistake, he'd reward you, give you an M & M; and if you were playing a LOUD mistake, he'd give you two. Go for it! The only mistake is being tentative.

— 731 —

"You're Just in Love," "I Wonder Why" from *Gypsy*, or "Anything You Can Do, I Can Do Better" from *Annie Get Your Gun* (Lerner & Lowe). Write a sassy answer, two oppositional points of view in a duet.

— 732 —

You're calling someone who's not there.

— 733 —

There's a merging of the worlds: the world of the senses, the world of the emotions, the world of thoughts, the spiritual world. How are these brought together in you? At the headwaters of your being, who are you? Bill Mann said, "I don't HAVE a soul, I AM a soul."

— 734 —

Refrigerator magnet poetry: a "chance" meeting of meaningful words. Well, okay. Word combinations are there to savor and might lead to a pretty (prettier) refrigerator at least. An example of this is "I'm an Alligator" on the Ziggy Stardust album (and movie) by David Bon Monage. He pulled phrases out of a box and arranged them at random.

— 735 —

I started to skip this idea because the concept bugs me, but so many people have had hits with the rivalry and sexual jealousy theme, I thought I'd at least mention it.
(Yes, you could go there, but why?)

"The Girl is Mine" (Paul McCartney)
"Jolene" (Dolly Parton)
"The Fool" (Maria Cannon, Gene Ellsworth, Charlie Stefl)
"Women Be Wise" (Sippy Wallace)

— 736 —

Write about your front porch, or on it.
"If the World Had a Front Porch" (Paul Nelson and Kenny Beard)

— 737 —

Ugh, "Back to the Cave." (Skip Ewing and Tim Johnson)
Write about a Neanderthal point of view.

— 738 —

Urge someone to stay in school, not to commit suicide, etc. Talk to some teenager in a song about something heavy.

— 739 —

There are four sections in a raga corresponding to changing seasons and spiritual growth. You could do the same in either your song structure or playing a single string to indicate the next movement in something that's through-composed.

— 740 —

Get in a boat. Row, sail, or float your way to tranquility, and let the water slapping on the sides of the boat give you a tempo.

— 741 —

Let Shakuhachi (Japanese bamboo flute), Peruvian pipes, ocarinas, Tuvan throat-singing, or some other unusual ways of "blowing" notes inspire you. Jeff Coffin, for instance, plays two sax reeds at once, and Sam Hinton could play a small harmonica from inside his mouth—with his lips closed!

— 742 —

Check out Italian production directions and put something together that takes one or more of them seriously: con brio, andante, ritardando, allegretto, misterioso, largo, piano forte, pianissimo.

— 743 —

Write un-metered music. Play something robato.

— 744 —

Cross-rhyme, where the syllable at the end of one line rhymes with a syllable in the middle of the line following it as in a poem by Rolphe Humphries from Babbette Deutsch's *Poetry Handbook*:

"Sing them low, or sing them soft.
Such a little while is left
To counterpoint the soundless drift of time,
Let rhyming fall and lift"

— 745 —

I wrote a bluegrass song with Mark Simos called "Silver and Gold" based upon a saying from the *Analects of Confucius*. The idea in Confucius was, "A man of words is silver; a man of deeds is gold." Our song said, "A smooth talkin' man is silver / A hard workin' man is gold." My friend Jimmy Jackson went to Korea and Japan with his country band and I asked him what they liked over there. He said they liked "I'm Just an

Old Lump of Coal (but I'm gonna be a diamond some day)" by Billy Joe Shaver. They said that it was a "very profound American lyric." "Very well," I said, "I'm going to write a country song for Asian people too." But try as I might, "I'm just an old grain of sand but I'm going to be a pearl some day" just wasn't cutting it. So I had the brilliant idea of looking into Asian proverbs themselves and you know what? I didn't exhaust them. There are loads of pearls of wisdom there for you to harvest. Let the proverbs of Iu Mein from Laos be another pearl bed for you. He wrote an alphabet book of proverbs called *Yiu Mienh Nzagh Mac Sou*, and if you don't get something out of it, well, you just haven't read it.

— 746 —

Put a mission statement or a little affirmation on a piece of paper. Tape it up somewhere you can see if often. If you keep a notebook—you DO keep a notebook, don't you?—you could put your affirmation on the cover. How about

I have something to say.
I'm here, showing God a good time.
Beauty matters, Truth matters.
I stand with the believers.
Great songs started here.

— 747 —

Commit to making time to write or co-write and put it on your calendar.

Write it in ink, set it in stone.

— 748 —

"A year after your death . . ."

Czeslaw Milosz, the great Nobel-prize-winning poet started a poem out this way. How does your life affect other people in it and how would you like it to?

— 749 —

Keys, doorways, halls, balcony, a summerhouse.
Standing in a doorway.

— 750 —

Write about the time somebody said to you:

Why can't you sleep?
What keeps you up at night?
When I awoke the next morning . . .

— 751 —

Write about a wound, a scar that won't heal, bruises, scrapes,
the scrapes you got into.

— 752 —

What was a time you found out about something
you weren't supposed to know?

What was a forbidden activity? What rules did you break, if any?

— 753 —

Shadows. What are yours?

— 754 —

Tell about the contents of a closet, dresser drawer, or locket.
When you opened the box . . .

— 755 —

Finish these:

At the end of the day _____.
This is not about _____.

— 756 —

What was the sky you were born under like?
Were there any special events coinciding with your birthday?

— 757 —

What are things you know without asking?

— 758 —

Sometimes she forgets . . .
What she wants
What things women know about love
What things men know about love
What things men/women don't know about love

— 759 —

Write about a wild-eyed dream.

— 760 —

What was the night sky like? What can you see by moonlight?
By starlight?

— 761 —

Who gave you flowers?

— 762 —

Write a song about being famous or being obscure. Chris Rock, joking about race relations, said, "It's pretty cool being famous…It's almost like being white." Randy Newman wrote, "It's Lonely at the Top," and Mike Dowling wrote a song in response: "It's Lonely at the Bottom, Too."

— 763 —

Mention a tattoo.

— 764 —

Write about recklessness, wild abandon.

— 765 —

It wasn't what she expected.
Write about a surprise, pleasant or unpleasant.

— 766 —

This is where I went wrong.

— 767 —

Write about a time you won big.

— 768 —

Write about a relief—something you didn't have to do after all.

— 769 —

"You must be unintimidated by your own thoughts."—Nikki Giovanni

— 770 —

Write about stealing something: a justifiable sin.

— 771 —

"I'm a promise broken . . ." (Derek Rutten)
Write the bad guy's tale.

— 772 —

Make use of the circle of 5ths, at least part of it:

"Hey, Good Lookin'" (Hank Williams)
"You've Got a Friend" (Carole King)
"You Send Me" (Sam Cooke)

— 773 —

Theodore Roethke said, "I remember how it was to drive in gravel."
Have you ever slung gravel by driving fast down a country road?

Brad Paisley's "Mud on the Tires"

— 774 —

You're caught in the act.

— 775 —

What didn't you do?

— 776 —

Write about being in bad company, small rebellions, e.g., "Young" by
Craig Weismann or "John Deere Green" (Dennis Lind).

— 777 —

Write from the middle out. Try starting from the end backwards, the
chorus first, the last line first, even the second or third verse first.

— 778 —

Write your own ring tones or a jingle for your voice mail.

Ask, "What are you up to?" My friend Eliot Smith copied, "I Want to be Seduced," by Gary Tigerman and sung by Leon Redbone on his answering machine and most of the people who called thought it was funny (except his parents—oops).

— 779 —

What would you trade? What wouldn't you trade?
What would you change? What wouldn't you change?

Do you believe that movement of a butterfly's wing in Indonesia is felt in Mexico?

— 780 —

What will you miss when you die?

— 781 —

Write about a town you passed through.

— 782 —

Your father's hands. His car, overalls, nervous tics, booze.
"The Suit" (Hugh Prestwood)

— 783 —

You ran out of time.

"In a week or two I was gonna buy her diamonds and a long, long string of pearls . . ." (Gary Burr and James House).

— 784 —

Overwrite; instead of putting a period at the end of a line, put a comma. Try chaining verses, writing a ten-minute song you plan on later editing.

— 785 —

"You build a novel the way you do a pyramid. One word, one stone at a time, underneath a full moon when the fingers bleed."—Kate Braverman

— 786 —

You're absent from your ordinary life. You're not at home. What does it feel like to be far from home?

— 787 —

Write while crying. Let it blotch up your page, smear your ink, gum up your keys; don't stop. Robert Frost once said, "No tears in the writer, no tears in the reader."

— 788 —

Finish: I still don't know . . .

— 789 —

Who has dubious intentions?

— 790 —

When did you change your mind?

— 791 —

Judy Reeves recommends changing perspective, fresh positioning, using someone else's style. You may like it better. Here are some sample writing positions:

Standers—Ernest Hemingway, Thomas Wolfe, Virginia Woolf, Lewis Carroll
Lie-ers down—Robert Lewis Stevenson, Mark Twain, Truman Capote
Bathtub soakers—Benjamin Franklin, Diane Ackerman
In the nude—D. H. Lawrence, Victor Hugo, Benjamin Franklin
Long walkers—Henry David Thoreau, Isaac Bashevis Singer, Wallace Sterns, Brenda Ueland, William Wordsworth, Carl Sandburg, Charles Dickens, and may I add Michael Smith, Steve Gillette, Chuck Cannon, Tia Sillers, Mike Reid, Allen Shamblin, Bob DiPiero. And, practically every songwriter in Jill Wood's book, *Successful Songwriters Secrets*, mentioned walking.

— 792 —

In the woods
Through the woods
Just beyond the edge of the woods
In the thickets
Lost in the wilderness
Tangled branches

— 793 —

Write about poison. What do you hope they do or
don't find the antidote for?

"I hope they never find the antidote for love." (Clive Gregson)

— 794 —

What was it that made something terrible? Difficult? Painful?
Sobbed like a child when you flew into a rage.

— 795 —

Meeting someone for the first time, you . . .

— 796 —

"Writing is not like parenting; torment, confusion, obstacles, and catastrophes are good things."—Rómelda Shaffer

— 797 —

Travel outside your continent, rhythmically. Typically, Celtic music emphasizes the 1st and 3rd beats of a 4-beat measure, and American music emphasizes the 2nd and 4th beats (back beats). But Middle Eastern music emphasizes the up beats on the 1/8th notes in between the 1 and 2, 3, and 4.

— 798 —

You're blindfolded. You're in the dark. Feel some objects without looking at them. Squint, plug your ears. What did you glance out of the corner of your eye? On what occasions were you blind, deaf? To what?

— 799 —

Write about a year ago.

— 800 —

You're one with another woman/man.

— 801 —

Use sculpting or painting to give you working methods.
Water it down.
Rough it up.
Polish it.
Paint it another color.

— 802 —

When did you want to throw in the towel?
When did you want to leave, but couldn't?

"To be a good writer, you not only have to write a great deal, you have to care."—Anne Lamott

— 803 —

Write about:
Circling the edge
Sitting on the edge
Falling

— 804 —

The moon is full. There is no moon. Mercury is in retrograde.

— 805 —

He's/she's wearing my ring. She takes it off. He puts it on.

— 806 —

A heat wave. A cold snap.

— 807 —

Write down a premonition.

— 808 —

Write in another genre, e.g., a movie treatment (a screenplay synopsis), a children's book, a how-to manual, a sermon, a story board, a want ad.

See if you can put the contents or the occasion back in song form.

— 809 —

Out-bully the critic. Rattle your saber. Judge the judge. Scare the pants off your naysayers. Toss the garbage. Tear apart. Set ablaze. Shut your self-doubt's business down. Grrr. Whack 'em. Lop the heads off dandelions.

"Blow 'Em Away" (Chuck Brodsky)

— 810 —

Someone/something is calling your name. Who? What?

"Highway" by Irene Kelley and Claire Lynch

— 811 —

Write about an abandoned house. A ghost town. A shell.

— 812 —

Write about a reflection.

— 813 —

The ebb tide.

— 814 —

Finish: One day . . .

— 815 —

If you have to make a choice between being a good boy
or girl, and being a . . .

— 816 —

It's too soon to tell. What is?

— 817 —

Study roadmaps for place names. I have a friend who is compiling a collection of songs about towns in Texas. I'll bet it's going to be a terrific songbook.

— 818 —

Predictability/unpredictability.
Things you do every day. The day everything changed.

— 819 —

Use "then," "anyway," "besides," "but," connecting run-on sentences and paragraphs, parenthetical phrases, lists and dashes.

Meander, "write a lot without a destination."—Natalie Goldberg

— 820 —

Avoidances. Defenses.
How do you spot them? How do people avoid the truth?

Changing the subject
Abandoning the starting place, dropping the old for the new, not writing
Going on about meaningless details
Closing up
Becoming glib
Being nice
Leaving the scene
Bringing in outside forces
Deus ex machina suddenly
Phony smile
Filling the gap
Bringing in a host of distracting characters/company
Using generalities instead of specifics
Hurrying along
Looking the other way
Ignoring the naked emperor, the man behind the curtain,
the elephant in the living room
Glossing over the top, like a coat of whitewash or wax
Affecting an attitude
Posing
Tap dancing around the topic
Killing the messenger

— 821 —

Take risks. Tell your secrets.

Willa Cather said, "Artistic growth is more than it is anything else, a refining of the sense of truthfulness."

"Truth is such a rare thing. It is delightful to tell it."—Emily Dickenson

— 822 —

Adventure. Wander neighborhoods you're unfamiliar with, routes home you haven't taken before. Lose your bearings—not so lost they have to send out the dogs, but lost enough so you're uncertain of exactly where you are or how to find your way home again. Travel a different road when you don't recognize landmarks, veer off in a direction you haven't gone before or in which you don't know what to expect. Get off the beaten path. Venture into the wilds—streets, shops, flora, fauna, architecture, geography.

Be a tourist.

— 823 —

You hear a siren.

— 824 —

Witness:
. . . before I was born
My real name is . . .
Once when I . . .
Afterward, I thought . . .

— 825 —

Write about being on the outside. You're standing on one side of a closed door.

— 826 —

Write about something that came in a box.

— 827 —

When the dust settled . . .

— 828 —

Write about an island.

— 829 —

These are the doubts I had . . .

— 830 —

If you could be like a character in a René Magritte painting and see the back of your own head, what would you write about from that oblique perspective? Don't look head on. Use a mirror. Stephen King says dreams help you do that. You don't face your experience head-on. You stylize from the back, like a hairdresser.

— 831 —

Who did you meet at a bar? A party?

— 832 —

Who in your life played a musical instrument
and what did it mean to him or her?

"Mandolin Rain" (Bruce Hornsby and John Hornsby)

— 833 —

Write about small change:

"Coin of the Realm" (Lisa Aschmann and Mark Simos)
"Nickels and Dimes" (Joe Vinikow)
"Nickels and Dimes and Love" (Stephen Lewis Clark and Fred Aylor McRae
performed by Vern Gosdin and John Michael Montgomery)

— 834 —

Write about the random possibility of miracles, signs,
portents, patterns, serendipity.

— 835 —

When were you in a state of surrender?

— 836 —

What is the sound of loneliness?

— 837 —

"Think of yourself as an incandescent power, illuminated, perhaps, and forever talked to by God and His messengers."—Brenda Ueland

— 838 —

Kiss your frogs.

— 839 —

What was inevitable? Meant to be? Fated?
So it has come to this.

— 840 —

What makes you feel reverent? Or is it the everyday? "Everything is Holy Now" (Peter Mayer), "Life is a Church" (Marcus Hummon)

— 841 —

What was a dream you gave up? Go back and reclaim it as possible.

— 842 —

"Throw away the lights (the definitions) and sing of what you see in the dark."—Wallace Stevens

— 843 —

Stand by yourself. What did you *mean* at the time? How dare you! Quelle how not to dare. Oh, why not?

— 844 —

Chaos, confusion, disarray. What's out of place?

— 845 —

"I will not reason and compare. My business is to create."—William Blake.

Enter a writing contest or a battle of the bands if you think it helps provoke your writing. But remember: you are idiosyncratic, unrepeatable, incomparable, indefinable, isolate and peerless.

— 846 —

The suitcase you/he/she packed.

— 847 —

Put a 5 chord at the end of a 4 bar phrase. Go 1 → 5, and then resolve another 4 bars with 5 → 1. In other words, use a false cadenza in the middle of your tune, and then resolve it with a real one.

— 848 —

Regarding description: "Starve it down—and make it run."—Marianne Moore

— 849 —

Use a rhyming dictionary, thesaurus. Wander.

— 850 —

Get rid of the words was, had, has, would be, subjunctive or passive verbs.

— 851 —

Dominate. Who is subjugated? What? Why? How?

— 852 —

What eclipses what? Who has given away his or her power?
How do they get it back?

— 853 —

When we made love . . . How was it?

— 854 —

I was listening to something I'd heard before . . .

— 855 —

"Good art is a form of prayer."—Fredrich Busch.
Do you agree?

The etymology for inspiration is taking God in. Breathe and write; write and breathe. Transcribe your spiritual epiphanies.

— 856 —

Do genre melding. Take some strong melodic tributaries and blend them until they're unrecognizable. An example that worked for my friend Rob Heath: "Smells Like Teen Spirit" (Nirvana) plus "Diamonds Are a Girl's Best Friend" (Leo Robin and Jule Styne). The equivalent sum sounds a little like the *Moulin Rouge* soundtrack.

— 857 —

Send your singer out on an errand.

"When your lover leaves you with the laundry." (Mike Williams)

— 858 —

Write about what's on the other side. The distant shore.

— 859 —

Take a walk.
Take a shower.
Wash the dishes.
Sweep the path.
Rake the leaves.
Take a nap.
Copy pages.
Go to a café.
Change your clothes.
Make a deadline. Remove a deadline.
Read a lyric passage or poem out loud.
Go to the library, the movies, a friend's house.
Cool off. Read your email. Do your homework.
Start with one concrete detail and follow it.

— 860 —

At the other end of the street, the dark end of the street, the other side of the tracks. Where are you? What happens?

— 861 —

You pick up a hitchhiker. Hop a train.

— 862 —

Rage. Collect several aspects of modern life that dismay you into one disenchanted warning, e.g. "The Eve of Destruction" by P. F. Sloan, "It's a Long Road Out of Eden" (Eagles).

— 863 —

Pay attention to everything that is one color. Yellow, red, blue, green.

— 864 —

Notice everything that is dying.
Notice everything that is new and fresh.

— 865 —

What is attracting, rejecting, magnetic, electrical, aligned? Confluences.

— 866 —

You are going anyway, in spite of . . .

John Ford Coley and I once wrote a song about a character who flips a coin to see whether she stays or goes. She decides to ignore the toss. "Heads or tails, heads, I'm going anyway."

— 867 —

Gillian Welch and I talked once about characters, issues, and scenes that recur with us. She spoke of her friend who wrote dozens of songs about the moon. My friend Dan Marcus and I share the oddity that our first songs were about pies. Gillian said she seemed to be a poor sharecropper in her songs. Sometimes we have recurring images.

Go with your issues and style. If something has use for you, keep milking it, take it on, use it up, wear it out.

— 868 —

Write about taking a detour. A dangerous ride.

— 869 —

Spend it all.
Shoot it.
Play it.
Lose it.

All _____
Right away _____
Every time.—Annie Dillard

— 870 —

What can never be said?

— 871 —

To be libeled, a person has to prove that by your writing you intend harm.

To be libeled, someone is falsely accused and is harmed. But you can justly accuse wrong-doers. Play the edge of disclosure. Jay Mankita has a song that is intentionally political but non-specific: "They lied, they lied . . . everybody knows they lied." Eric Schwarz has a song in which he sings, "I'm going to sit on a hornet's nest . . ." The inference is clear without being libelous.

— 872 —

This is where I come from . . .
This is where I belong . . .
My body is . . .
His/her body is . . .

"Write in recollection and amazement for yourself."—Jack Kerouac

— 873 —

Specificity is generosity. Be generous with your senses and your details.

Sycamore, eucalyptus, willow, pine (not just tree).
Honeysuckle, roses, irises, lilies—use the language of flowers.

— 874 —

When was the first time you thought differently from your family?

— 875 —

Comings and goings.
Look in your neighbors' windows, shops, office buildings.
Speculate.

— 876 —

Write a bunch of clichés and then write away from them instead with the most off-the-wall turns of phrase and comparisons you can think of. Write about petty crime, faux pas, and second thought as opposed to impulses. Avoid clichés like the plague.

— 877 —

When did someone go too far?

— 878 —

Have a serious chat with a chair.
Talk to your dog, a baby, a cat, your goldfish—to those
who cannot understand.

Thoreau is said to have had conversations with woodchucks.

— 879 —

Hans Christian Andersen put a sign next to his bed that said, "I Am Not Really Dead." How do you know you aren't?

— 880 —

Brew coffee. Make bread. Burn candles. Sniff rosemary, orange, lilac. Dust with lemon oil. Set the stage for writing by smelling up the house.

— 881 —

Find your tribe. Hang out with songwriters.

— 882 —

Make writing or co-writing a marathon. See how long you can keep at it at a stretch.

— 883 —

Write about the time the lights went out.

— 884 —

Write about skin. Where you live.

— 885 —

Make lists.
These are the things to trust:
These will always disappoint:
This is where you can always go:

— 886 —

À la Robert Fulghum, what did you learn in kindergarten?
Ponder and observe children at play. What do you see?

— 887 —

Say what things look like besides what they are. Think of function rather than form or form rather than names. Edward de Bono and James Lowell Adams recommended this as a creative design technique. Richard Feynman talked about how knowing the name of a thing teaches us so little about it, it's better to stay away from naming anything at all while studying it. These creative engineers/physicists have good advice for songwriters as well.

— 888 —

Look at your shadow—your dark side.

_____was a mistake.
_____are my weaknesses.

— 889 —

That was as far as I could go. How far was that?

— 890 —

Write about a pillow, a bed, a bath, or a shower.
"Slide off of your satin sheets." (Wayne Carson and Donn Tankersly)
"Send me the pillow that you dream on."(Hank Locklin)

— 891 —

Consider some benchmarks:

Emily Dickinson wrote 1,800 poems.
(Seven of them were published in her lifetime.)
Mozart wrote twelve enduring pieces of music before he was five.
Van Gogh painted eight hundred pictures (and sold one in his lifetime.)
Anthony Trollope wrote forty-seven novels and sixty short stories. He started writing when he was forty. That's twelve million words.
Leo Tolstoy rewrote *War and Peace* eight times.
Tim O'Brien writes every day.
Don Schlitz writes every day. He co-wrote two number-one songs with Beth Nielsen Chapman one day before lunch.
Steve Allen wrote more than seven hundred published songs and had eight-thousand songs when he died.
Get the point? Get the picture? You can do more, more, more.

— 892 —

I would especially like to encourage older songwriters to start and/or persist in their craft. Consider these benchmarks:

Picasso and Georgia O'Keefe painted into their eighties.
P. G. Wodehouse wrote stories in his nineties.
Bob Hope and George Burns wrote jokes and memoirs in their hundredth year.

— 893 —

The possible causes of and solutions to writer's block:

Looking to expectations and perfectionism. Bar set too high? Lower it.

Fear of failure, fear of success, fear of finishing. (Address these, maybe with a counselor.)

Fear of confrontation—fear of the emotional material itself. (Now that's your juiciest stuff to write about.)

Maybe the form or the genre doesn't fit the material, the mold you think it does.

Reshape the piece or change the mold. AABA to ABAB structure, up tempo to ballad, not a song at all?

Trying to fit yourself into a mold? Reiner Maria Rilke wrote: "One may do anything; this alone corresponds to the whole breadth life has. But one must be sure not to take it upon oneself out of opposition, out of spite toward hindering circumstances or with others in mind, out of some kind of ambition."

Check your motives for writing. Don't be ambitious, going against the grain to prove something. Be playful.

A sense of being overwhelmed—feels like you bit off more than you can chew. Write your song note-by-note word-by-word, line-by-line.

Excuse yourself from the charts, the biggest divas, etc.

Lifestyle and work habits gone awry? Call a H.A.L.T. when you're hungry, angry, lonely or tired. Get water, breathing, exercise, good food, and sleep into the picture. Some songwriters are extremely careful. Keith Little, for example, only eats natural, raw food. He says it gives him loads of stamina for touring.

Inventory your stressors and distractions such as divorce, illness, job loss, relocation.

Maybe expecting yourself to write with worries on your mind is just adding another worry. Give yourself some slack.

— 894 —

Reread your automatic writing, your practice page, your discarded notes on other songs. Mine them.

— 895 —

These are the lies I told you:
These are the things I kept from you:
I'm willing to come clean about:
This is how I really feel/felt:

— 896 —

What's worth having, seeking, doing?

— 897 —

What will happen that can't be stopped?

— 898 —

What "goes without saying"?
What "was left behind"?
Who proposed what to you?

— 899 —

Write about yearning.

— 900 —

"You Put a Spell on Me" (Greg Spence Wolf)
"Witchy Woman" (Eagles)
"(Must be the) Season of the Witch" (Donovan Leitch)

— 901 —

A new day is dawning. The sun is rising. What do you make of that?

— 902 —

Susan Wooldridge and I like the idea of going through reference books
and manuals to find words and ideas: houses repair, woodworking, field
guides, car repair, cookbooks, pottery books, birds of the Pacific Coast,
inter-tidal invertebrates, Appalachian wildflowers, fly fishing lures, bats,
butterflies, sewing, glass blowing books.

I once wrote down the names of fresh water lures found in a store in West Texas just in case a song about fishing comes up someday.

Their names were evocative and sounded like country song titles to me.

— 903 —

Notice menus, marquee signs, bus boards, billboards, what is said in chat rooms. Jamey Whiting and I wrote songs off of titles we got from a church marquee near his home. We wrote, "Feed the Faith, Starve the Doubt" and went to lunch. On the way back we noticed that the deacon had changed the marquee.
It now read, "Only Jesus will satisfy."

— 904 —

Write about divine intervention, spirit, angels, messengers, appointments, annunciations.

— 905 —

Coffee or tea?

Have your singer have a cup of Joe or so. Joni Bishop and I wrote "Buzzed" in Starbucks and Ellen Britton and I wrote a song called, "Oh, Joe," which is a love song to coffee. My favorite part went: "They say tall, dark, and handsome is every young girl's dream, but without the thrill you give me, mere looks don't amount to a hill of beans."

— 906 —

Are you pissed off? Are you hot? Go ahead. Mention the unmentionable, the unprintable words, the way you'll never get it on the radio. The lil' sneaky ways to circumlocate and circumnavigate the problem. Say it anyway a different way.

— 907 —

Write a portrait of yourself in a social context.
First person, present tense.
Third person, obituary-style, past tense.
Second person, looking in the mirror.

Consider how your friends might describe you or introduce you and how you would do that for them. How is it that you and he/she belong together? How are you alike/complimentary? "Tonight I'm Looking for a Party Crowd" by Jimbeau Hinson and David Lee Murphy. "I'm the king of fools, where's my crown," by Fred Knobloch.

— 908 —

Try writing a strong song by writing the narrative out in prose, first as either a short story or a plot outline. Try different endings. Can you withhold information and have a surprise ending? At what point should the realization occur to the singer? Don Wayne is a master of this type of song, e.g. "Saginaw Michigan."

— 909 —

The happy couple, the just desserts . . . Jonathan Byrd has a character hide diamonds in the back of a (hocked) stereo. Is there another character you could write from? Is there a theme in your writing you could explore more fully or break out of? Can you find humor or uplift in a tragic story?

— 910 —

Get song ideas from jobs and verbs:

Wash, style, trim, cut, color, comb
Fry, sauté, chop braise, baste, bake
Mix, stir spackle, brush, stroke, roll, tape
Dig, spade, plant, transplant, hoe, weed

— 911 —

Where do rivers join, boundaries converge, roads cross? How about when you've come to the fork in the road? The top of the hill/heap? The bottom?

— 912 —

Wislawa Szymborska, Nobel-prize-winning poet said, "The window had other views."

What other views did yours have?

— 913 —

Start on the 5 of the scale.

"Blue Moon" (Richard Rodgers and Lorenz Hart)
"Since I Fell For You" (Buddy Johnson)
"Heart and Soul" (Hoagy Carmichael and Frank Loesser)

— 914 —

On a blank piece of paper write,
"What I want to write a song about is _____."
Fill it in.

— 915 —

Make lists like:

Fifty questions I'd like answers to
Fifty things I don't want to forget
Three people I admire
Three meanest sumbitches
Three times I wished the ground would open up and swallow me
Three things I'd love to tell the Nosey Parkers of this town

— 916 —

Time is short. Write about what you would do with

"One More Day" (Steve Dale Jones and Neil Thrasher)

— 917 —

What is a hesitation or reluctance you have?

These were the reasons to stay: _____.
These were the reasons to leave: _____.

— 918 —

Ask one of your dreams for help. Rilke wrote, "Ask yourself in the quietest hour of your night: 'Must I write?' Dig down in yourself for the deep answer. And if this should be in the affirmative, if you may meet this solemn question with a strong smile, I must, then build your life accordingly to this necessity."

— 919 —

What are the avenues of escape? Karen Taylor-Good and I wrote a song about going off "into the wild blue yonder."

— 920 —

What's haunted in your life? Is it a used car as in "Private Malone" (Wood Newton and David Ball), a sofa, a birdcage, a grape arbor?

— 921 —

You had to refuse an invitation. Why?

— 922 —

Finish: ". . . and nobody objected."

— 923 —

Invite your bad self to talk. What does the devil on your shoulder want you to do? Tell that old biddy off? Sleep 'til noon? Flirt with somebody on the off-your-list list? Hijack a rocket, fill an ocean liner, break curfew, raid the pantry?

— 924 —

Write about a late-night phone call. Paul Sanchez wrote a moving Christmas song about the car accident report on Christmas. Then there's the person you just couldn't wait to see or talk to, the cry for help, the sweaty sheets.

— 925 —

Write about seeing someone for the last time.

Nora Ephron's dying mother said, "Take note, it's all copy."

— 926 —

Why writers write: Marcel Proust said, "This life, that at every moment we distort, can be restored to its true pristine shape . . . within the confines of a book." (or a song)

— 927 —

What color was their hair? How did that affect your relationship?
The blonde, the redhead, the bald eagle.

— 928 —

Forget the song you want to write. Focus on ONE at a time—the one
at hand, the part of one at hand, the title at the top of the list, the lyric
at the top of the pile.

— 929 —

What is something you want but can't have?

— 930 —

We stopped at the nearest diner by the side of the road. All we had was
chili, chips. We ate Chinese. We cooked that here and on a spit. When
was food unimportant? Important?

— 931 —

Describe the last light of day, a secret collection, a whole life of madness.

— 932 —

Take any triad (major, minor, diminished, or augmented) and play it with your right hand over your left-handed chords. You're already improvising. Triads over minor 2 5 1 as in Bill Evans' "Beautiful Love" Em7♭5 → A7alt → Dm6 progression, or "Giant Steps" by John Coltrane Bmaj7 → D7 → Gmaj7 → B♭7 → Emaj7 → Am7 → D7 → Gmaj7 → B♭7 → E♭maj7 → F♯7 → Bmaj7 → Fm7 → B♭7, etc. Alternating major and minor triads descending in whole steps gives rise to new melodies over these rapid changes. I got this from an article called, "Get a Sophisticated Sound From a Simple Technique" by Andy LaVerne.

— 933 —

Practice slurring notes and repeating notes on your keyboard or guitar. With slurred notes, vary the volume of the attack, right versus left hand, inner versus outer strings, notes in each triad. When you're restringing your guitar, play with the tuners, the slack and tighter strings. What mood are you in? John Tirro, James Thiele, and I wrote the song, "Un-strummed Guitar," whose premise was: Without God, no music.

— 934 —

Go back and forth, upscale and down, between major and minor 6ths like Thelonious Monk did in "Misterioso." Harold Danko calls it developing "hand embouchure" when you do this fast: C → E7 → A7 → Dm → E7 → A7 → D7 → G7 → C → E7, etc., and then melodically you get all sorts of possibilities against this progression, not to mention warmed-up hands.

— 935 —

Take any existing melody and rearrange it. Run C & W took soul R & B music and made it all bluegrass, for instance. This has the effect of helping you get inside a genre. It's making a parody of the music rather than of the lyrics. Then backtrack and parody the lyrics, the opposite of #698. Pay tribute to one genre by rearranging it in another. "Moody Bluegrass" was a project of Dave Harvey's. He arranged the Moody Blues songs into bluegrass, and Larry Cordle arranged Lynyrd Skynyrd songs into bluegrass. Larry's next bluegrass originals reflected the influence of Lynryd Skynyrd's Southern rock.

— 936 —

Sound black, sound white, sound Hispanic. Take racial and cultural musical styling, copy and exaggerate somebody else's. Tom Kimmel and I wrote a song about people who do that called, "Copy Cat."

— 937 —

Choose objects like chewing gum, beard, and truck stop.
Put three in a song.

How about letter, window, table?
Skates, lake, sunrise.

— 938 —

Check out the biographies of session bands.
What were they doing before they got signed?

— 939 —

Try Fado, like Flamenco, with a 5/8 time signature.
Work with dramatic, declaratory love songs from the Portuguese.

— 940 —

Watch less television. Surrendering your will to this external thing that
demands less-to-no attention span, can crimp your creative output. Be
a producer, not a consumer; be an active, not a passive person; a maker,
not a receiver of culture.

— 941 —

Here's a quote from Niels Bohr who gave us a
pretty picture of a hydrogen atom:
"If an idea does not appear bizarre, there is no hope for it."

— 942 —

Go to the place where you can be king (only without the beheadings, as
Michael Smith would say). You rule. What's going on in *your* domain?

— 943 —

Write about rebuilding.
How does a city heal itself?

What are the qualities of the people who rebuild: those who help the community after a disaster? Write stories for and about the rescue workers, the survivors.

What gets saved and what gets left behind?

— 944 —

Make a half step change to any note in a chord you are playing. Listen to the way chords morph into each other. Move very slowly stepwise.

— 945 —

Make contrapuntal motion between the melody and the bass line. Bach, Wes Montgomery, Joe Beck, and George Van Eps are people to go to school on in this regard.

— 946 —

Tell the story of the ripple effect, cascade, avalanche, dominos, snowball or paying it forward.

— 947 —

Write about the bridge, the fourteenth story, the train trestle, the speedway, the suicide stance. What is it? Write the note in song. Argue for life or death (or do both). A duet?

— 948 —

Embellish.

Break out of simple chords to extended chords to walk a bass line.

G → G maj7, Gmaj6 → Gmaj9.

Or reduce.

Reduce extended chords to their basic chords.

Fmaj9 =Am7, C7♭9♯11= G♭7, C♯9 = G♭7♯5, C7B9 = Edim7, etc.

For instance, adding to a C triad chord the B making it Cmaj7, the D making it Cadd9, or C2. The D and B making it Cmaj9, etc. In general, every other note in the scale will effectively embellish a chord.

This exercise will give rise to some great progressions you can use.

C 1

E 3

G 5

B 7

D 9 or 2

F 11 or 4

A 13 or 6

Use altered chord types like Cm9 → Cmaj9 in "I Think I'm Going Out of My Head." (Teddy Randazzo and Bobby Weinstein)

Here's a good song that models the use of extended chords: "Through the Fire" by David Foster, Cynthia Weil and Chaka Khan.

— 949 —

Displace the melodic motif you have going by an eighth note so that
you begin a musical phrase on an off-beat.

— 950 —

Vary note values so that you begin or hold a musical phrase in one section in a different place than you did the first time. Repeat a melodic motif twice as fast or slow as the first time you played or sang it.

— 951 —

Make one note in the first melodic phrase start the next one so that two phrases start and end in the same spot. Rounds often do this dovetailing, e.g., "Working on a Building" (trad.)

— 952 —

Money or honey?
Women who choose the honey and refuse the money:

"Peanuts and Diamonds" by Bill Anderson
"The Moon over Georgia" by Hugh Prestwood
"Silver Threads and Golden Needles" by A. P. Carter
Women who choose the money and are sad about it:
"Mansion on a Hill" (Hank Williams)
Men who promise the honey that's missing:
"Tight Fitting Jeans" (Conway Twitty)
"Satin Sheets" (Johnny Paycheck)
"Rose in Paradise" (Waylon Jennings)
"Crystal Chandeliers" (Charley Pride)

— 953 —

Use the same phrase rhythm three times. Then, put the title in a unique, different phrase rhythm so that it jumps out as the title. Pause before the title. Put the title in a lower or higher range than the rest of the melodic phrases as in "I Swear" (Frank Myers and Gary Baker). The melody line in the verse happens three times and so does the chorus three times plus different two lines in the hook or title, e.g., "Harder to Love," "This Love," "She Will Be Loved" (all 3 songs by Maroon 5). For another example in a different genre, listen to "You'll Think of Me" (Keith Urban), or songs where the two sections (verse and chorus) have the same melody notes and same rhythm but different chords. Music progresses as different song forms and melodic structures gain currency. In the 40's AABA (verse verse bridge verse) was popular; in the 60's ABAB (verse chorus verse chorus) gained popularity. In the 80's and 90's ABC ABC DC (verse pre-chorus chorus verse pre-chorus chorus bridge chorus) was popular. The above-mentioned $3A^+B$, $3A^+B$ melody, rhythm, and rhyme structure seems to be one of the current most popular forms. In this case, A is a line of melody, and B is a different line of melody, not a verse, bridge, or a chorus structure.

— 954 —

Mine hymns, folksongs, and nursery rhymes for classic melodic motifs to vary and build on as song kernels, or borrow from classical pieces. "Claire de Lune" was turned into a song by Melissa Javors. "St. Anne's Reel" was turned into a song by Wil Maring.

— 955 —

Use a nonsense syllable to stretch out your hook by exclaiming it.
Spend a lot of vocal time on the oohs and ahhs.

"Ooh baby I love your way" (Peter Frampton) and "Oh, I just fall in love again" (Steve Dorff, Larry Herbstritt, Gloria Sklerov, and Harry Lloyd)

— 956 —

Break up the phrase rhythm of a line in different ways and
repeat various words in it.

Jason Blume gives the following examples:
If you really, really, really love me.
If you, if you, if you really love me.

— 957 —

I don't write melodies on an instrument. Neither do Seal, Sting, or several other GRAMMY®-winning melody writers. Mel Brooks wrote the whole score to *The Producers* without an instrument. Try it and see if you like it as a method of writing. Singing over a pre-recorded a cappella part can give you additional harmony ideas.

— 958 —

Allen Shamblin and Mike Reid laugh about the original tempo and time signature of "I Can't Make You Love Me," the Bonnie Raitt hit.

Up-tempo, bouncy bluegrass didn't quite serve the lyric.
Go back and see if radically changing genres helps your writing.

— 959 —

Change one note only—high or low—to emphasize a hook. For example,

"I've Got Friends in Low Places" (Dewayne Blackwell and Bud Lee) empha-sizes the point of the song.

— 960 —

How do you get to a place? Give driving directions.

Steve Goody in the Weisenheimers has one for NASCAR driving:
"Take a left, take a left, take a left, go straight
Take a left, take a left, take a left, go straight"

— 961 —

Someone doubts your love. How do you respond?

"I see the questions in your eyes" from "I Swear" (Baker and Richardson)

— 962 —

Use more than one meaning of the hook.

"I Let Her Lie" (Tim Johnson) (To sleep and to prevaricate.)

— 963 —

Embarrass your audience. Make 'em squirm and titter as
Jon Inns did in "Daddy Cut the Big One in the Hornlake
Mississippi Missionary Baptist Church."

— 964 —

Make an incomplete sentence that is finished by the next line.

"Soon" (Casey Kelly and Bob Regan)

— 965 —

What are your favorite songs and why? Keep a list and
keep track of your reasons.

See if you can spot trends or commonalities and write a song that makes use
of one of them. For instance, I happen to like descending melodies in the chorus
(as in a lot of the Louvin Brothers' songs) and in songs (like theirs) that are instru-
mentally simple and very easy to harmonize vocally, so I deliberately set out to
write one like that.

— 966 —

Write new words to a Beatles tune and give them to a writing partner.
Don't tell them what song it was, and ask them to write a new melody
that fits those lyrics.

Clive Gregson likes to do this as a co-writing exercise.

— 967 —

Make an overall songwriting agenda or homework
assignment for yourself.

Cathy Fink and Marcy Marxer were asked to write songs about nutrition for kids. They put together a whole group of songs called "Bon Appetit."

I wrote songs for Earth Day about global warming, and Joyce Rouse has put together several projects based on her moniker, "Earth Mama."

— 968 —

Unlike your instruction in grade school to write about what
happened on your summer vacation, an even closer-to-the-mark
instruction would be: "Make me care about what happened to you
on your summer vacation."

— 969 —

Play word jazz.

At the end of a word, stick the last half of that word onto the next word, e.g., nowhere, where upon, pontoon, tune that guitar, tar and feather. Like stretching before pumping iron, these are warm-ups for songwriting. They're not songwriting itself; they're word games. Playing word games limbers you up for songwriting. Rob Heath used a computer program, www.ideafisher.com to chain the end words and the beginning words of familiar sayings together. He found 60,000 candidates for song titles this way.

— 970 —

Write a tune in which the melodic motifs are arranged: AABA in the verse and CDDC in the chorus, or a tune structure more like a fiddle tune, where the melodic motifs are structured: AABCCBABC. In other words, use repetition and variation on a theme in some very closely structured way, repeating motifs at regular intervals.

— 971 —

Meditate on saltwater, salt, wood, metal, weapons, or roads. In other words, what ubiquitous material with emotional resonance can you track throughout a general or personal history?

— 972 —

Think at the speed of swimming. Do laps and write in your head as you swim. You could also shoot baskets, play golf, etc. Popular songwriter retreats include river rafting.

— 973 —

Write an instruction manual for parents.
Call it *"A Parent's Home Companion: The Instruction Manual."*

After all, when you buy a new washer or refrigerator, there is one. Or, report back to your parents: "Dear Mom . . ."

— 974 —

Write a song in which the title appears only once—at the very end.

"Rock Salt and Nails" (Utah Phillips), "Boots of Spanish Leather" (Bob Dylan)

— 975 —

Rap some verses but keep the rest of the song melodic.

"It's a Spice World" (Spice Girls)
"I Wanna Talk About Me" (Toby Keith and Bobby Braddock)

— 976 —

Enact the behavior you're speaking of in a lyric. These puns were called Tom Swifties.

"I'm more judgmental than you are."
"I'll procrastinate tomorrow."
"I'm sorry I'm apologizing."

— 977 —

Here are some party games to get a good laugh and to loosen up your writing:

Filter everything downward. Say, sing, or write, "I like you" instead of "I love you," or substitute "I" for "you." For example, "When I close my eyes, I see me," "I do something to me," "I make me feel so beautiful." Michael Johnson does this well in "You make me feel so-so." Arrange songs in minor keys that are usually major, e.g., "Jingle Bells" as a dirge. Play ballads fast. Jon Yudkin has gypsy violin versions of country songs. They're not only hilarious, but creative.

— 978 —

Separate out your harmony and distribute the harmonies among the instruments completely, e.g., Howlin' Wolf, where a song is played with the bass on the 5 chord, the guitar on the 1 chord, and the keys on the 4 chord.

— 979 —

Use an "appogatura."

For example, 1 → 7 in "Yesterday" goes up over and down to a note in a chord from outside the chord.

— 980 —

Balance moments of repose with moments of agitation.

— 981 —

Arpeggiate all the notes of your song on the guitar, and follow it vocally exactly as Sting does in "Every Little Thing She Does is Magic."

— 982 —

Play guitar in open C, G, or D major tunings. They would be the following strings: DADF♯AD, DGDGBD, or CGCGCF. Play in parallel minor tunings: Dm, Gm, and Cm by lowering the third half a step in each of the above tunings, or raising that string half a step which gives you GSus 4 tunings, e.g., DSus4 (DADGAD), GSus4 and CSus4.

As Mark Simos said, "There is nothing holy about regular tuning." Kyser Capos makes partial capos that assist in alternate tunings (and has a DVD with Randall Williams that demonstrates). How many partial capos can you use on one song? Two? Three? Four?

— 983 —

There are so many lyric-writing tools available on the Internet. Here are six of them that might jog your bean: MasterWriter.com, phrasefinder.com, wordNet, rhymezone.com (a rhyming dictionary), rapdict.org (a rapper's dictionary), and http://dir.yahoo.comReference/ Dictionaries/Slang (a slang dictionary). I saw a sign a while back that read, "A good workman uses the right tool for the job." It's still true. While we're on the subject of using computers to write, Scipe (voice over Internet protocol) has been helpful in getting distant co-writers together in real-time. Okay, if that's not a songwriting idea, it's still a way to forage for ideas. Sampling music libraries is a great way to juxtapose one type of music with another quickly, or to hear twelve versions of the same song and compare them. Isolating arrangements, genres, playing styles, song forms, topics, etc. and collecting them for creative purposes has never been easier.

— 984 —

"I Will Always Love You" (Dolly Parton) is the title and the chorus words. That's all there is. Check it out; it's one way to simplify a song. Make the entire chorus lyric be your title and only the title.

— 985 —

"Girl, let's not be friends"
"Let's just be friends"
"Let's not just be friends"

Try changing a phrase with one or two words.

— 986 —

Play an alternating bass-driven series of bass notes: 1 1 4 4 2 5 1 5.

Start a song with straight eights and then try it swung. (Pushing ahead the third note in a 4-beat phrase and dropping a beat in the next-to-last measure.)

Do a finger slap on a bass, e.g., play A with the thumb, then B on the D string with the index finger, then E on the G string with the middle finger, rolling your wrist. Use this exercise as an ostinato (repeated pattern) to write a melody on top.

— 987 —

Write in an unusual mode like Mixolydian:

"You Learn" (Alannis Morrisette and Glen Ballard)
"Norwegian Wood" (John Lennon and Paul McCartney)

Or Dorian mode:
"Eleanor Rigby" (John Lennon and Paul McCartney)
Most of Carlos Santana's music is in Dorian mode.

Or Phrygian mode:
Lorena McKennit has an entire album called *Beneath a Phrygian Sky.*

— 988 —

Write a song regarding flying and personal freedom.

"I'm Like a Bird" (Nelly Furtado)
"I Believe I Can Fly" (R. Kelly)

— 989 —

There are three types of Bluegrass songs, according to Eddie Stubbs and
Dudley Cornell of the Johnson Mountain Boys:
Sorrowful
Pitiful
Morbid

According to the Irish guitarist and singer John Doyle, the basic song plot
of the great Celtic tradition is: Boy meets girl, boy gets girl, boy murders girl.
With suicide, murder and lost love being your available topics, what's the holdup?
We've got misery to dispense (and bemoan), jail to go to, etc.

— 990 —

Split the pacing of your writing into two or three occasions. Have as a goal only starting an idea on one day and developing it on another day, or separating the music and lyric writing for different occasions, with people involved, hours, days, or even weeks apart. Plan on not finishing it all in one go. Make use of your subconscious to work on it during your time away. And really take the heat off timetables. I was fond of saying to my kids, "Life is not a race." Neither is art.

— 991 —

Think of things you can do without. They're chicken skin. Chicken Skin. Hey, a song title! Your mis-locution of lyrics will tell you where your subconscious clarity and intentions are wavering. If need be, start over and separate music and lyrics to see where the natural prosody lies, or what parts you can get rid of. As Jody Stecher said, "I'm either the smartest dumb guy or the dumbest smart guy in the world." In your flustered self, you'll learn most from your own accidents, and stumbling toward a song is not an exception. What are your most precious humiliations and blunders?

— 992 —

Take advantage of your limitations.

When people ask my friend Nancy Conescu how she plays the guitar the way she does, she answers, "I take advantage of my limitations." Incorporate what's special and perhaps especially flawed into your style. "Thumbs" Carlisle and Jim Burrill taught themselves to play guitar like dobros (flat in their laps), and it works.

Don Jones plays finger-style guitar upside down and backward (left-handed), and it works. It always makes me smile to think that the Castillian accent spoken by millions was in the aftermath of a monarch with a speech impediment. You never know when you could be starting a trend.

— 993 —

Don't submit to "the tyranny of rhyme" as Robert Frost called it.

"Bridge Over Troubled Water" (Paul Simon) has only one rhyme in it, for instance. Try doing without any rhyme, or ration it sparingly.

— 994 —

Write about monsters, dragons. Retell a myth bringing in fantastic animals likes unicorns, gryphons, the phoenix, the golem, dinosaurs, Nessie, or centaurs.

— 995 —

Write songs in closely-related styles just by changing one or two elements. For instance, Ray Charles said that blues and gospel were pretty much the same. "In the blues you're singing, 'Oh, Baby,' and in gospel you're singing, 'Oh, Lord.'"

— 996 —

Treat music you hear on television or film as if it's the temporary music, that is, the music used by the film studio before the final music is licensed to give the music producers and film editors the general idea of how it will later work into a scene. Maybe your turn will come to replace it. Be very specific and restrict yourself in the genre and tempo so that you time- and date-stamp a scene. One of the things I love about writing music for film, is that "dated" is not an insult, it's a compliment.

— 997 —

Who's been overlooked today among the people you've encountered?

The bathroom attendant?
"She Works Hard for the Money" by Donna Summers
The car wash attendant?
"Car Wash" (Rose Royce)
"Working at the Car Wash Blues" (Jim Croce)
The cafeteria worker, the bus driver, the janitor, the phlebotomist? Gotcha!

— 998 —

Because the Bible tells me so. The Bible should never be underestimated as a source of lyrics. Further, pay attention to your minister or rabbi when they're saying pithy things.

— 999 —

If you did a concordance of words that most frequently appear in successful lyrics (besides the usual *heart, night,* and *if*), you will see that people often notice *tears, cry, sweet, only,* and *kiss* in the title.

—1000—

I used to say to my kids when I was contemplating a large purchase or making a rash decision, "*When* are we living? *When* are we living?" Their response was, "*Now*, Mama, *now*!" And then I'd go for it.

If you haven't gotten around to your creative life yet, here's something to spur you on: Tim Bays wrote "What Are You Waiting For?" His father asked him this question from a hospital bed when Tim was waffling over moving to Nashville to pursue his musician/songwriting dreams. His father's time was short (isn't ours too?) and his advice to his son was, "If I had a dream to do something, I'd get on with it if I were you."

What are you waiting for?

Appendix

There are five main elements, or tools, useful in songwriting: *form, melody, harmony, rhythm,* and *lyrics.* Because of this, I structured my course at PSGW to discuss these topics, in this order, one on each of the five days of my songwriting class. What follows is part of the course material. Don't be spooked if it looks technical. This is partly a glossary to help you find your way through the words in the idea section and partly a short introduction to songwriting per se. The words in the following informal glossary aren't alphabetized; rather, I've placed them in the order in which people are most likely to encounter these elements when they're writing a song. If you get a handle on these concepts, you can write songs. They're like building blocks; put one down and you can see where you can stack the next one. But I wouldn't dream of telling you *how* to write a song. I honestly don't know, and if I did know, I wouldn't say. Why? Because it would be a terrible box in which to put yourself if there were a recipe or an algorithm that you had to follow. Fortunately, there's no such thing. You're safe from pedagogy. Songwriting is nestled in the heart of creativity, where it belongs.

I have some unusual ways of conceptualizing this material. The way I write songs is a bit of a curiosity. People sometimes wonder how a musical ignoramus, a person who doesn't play an instrument, could compose songs. So, I've included a section about my own writing process that appears after this appendix. Of course, I'm also indebted to many wonderful musicians and co-writers who've helped me actualize songs. But it's not just sour grapes to say that you don't need musicianship or musicians to hear your music. You don't need a lot of "background." Waiting for yourself to be sufficiently prepared, for the day when you're really *qualified* to write songs—that day may never come, even with a Ph.D. in music. *Be* unready.

Allow for imperfection. Remain open to chaos. Your education can get in the way of your creativity. Ask any hardened veteran of grade school! Did you play more in kindergarten or in 12th grade? Most of us would answer the former, but what we need is *recess* for adults. So, take the "educational" part of this book with a grain of salt. The appendix is here to help, not hinder, your playing. It's really recess time, not class time that makes the difference.

LINGO REGARDING SONG FORM

Hook: the catchy part of a song.

Title: the name of the song; it often has the hook in it.

Chorus: the melodically repeated part of a song. The chorus is the "goal" of the song that sums it up or reflects the theme. The chorus usually has the hook in it. Because this is almost always the focal point of a song, it can be quicker to write it first and then backtrack to the other sections.

First verse: the section that motivates or sets up the situation or storyline that leads to the chorus.

Second verse: the plot thickens. The continuation of the storyline or another angle of approach to the chorus. Almost always musically identical to the first verse.

Bridge: a breath of fresh air, melodically and lyrically different from the rest of the song. The bridge takes a different approach to the song idea. For instance, if the rest of the song is a narrative and personal in tone, the bridge might be more philosophical in tone; or if the rest of the song is slow, the bridge might be faster. Frequently the bridge is signaled by a change in key that ramps the song up energetically into the last rousing chorus.

Intro: instrumental introduction to a song often containing part or all of a verse.

Outro: also known as the "tag"; instrumental conclusion to a song, often the same as the intro.

Song Forms:

If A = a verse

and B = a chorus or the next different section from the one preceding it,

and C = a bridge or the next different section from the one preceding it, here are some typical song forms:

ABAB: usually country or folk style, e.g., "O, Susannah."

ABABCB: the most common form; country, pop, and R & B style, e.g., Billy Cobham's "Soul Provider."

Intro, ABABCAB, outro: pop, rock, jazz; such as "Waiting for a Star to Fall" (George Merrill and Shannon Rubicam).

AA'BAA'BCB: a common pop and rock style where A' is a repeated change in verse, or *pre-chorus*, as in the Bee Gees' "High as a Mountain."

AABA: jazz and pop, e.g., "Yesterday" (Paul McCartney).

ABAC: jazz, for example, "All of Me" (Seymour Simons and Gerald Marks).

AAA: blues and bluegrass, e.g., "In the Pines" (Leadbelly).

BABAB: of course you can start with the chorus, but make sure it's not like giving away the punch line of a joke. Example: "Chain of Fools" (Donald Covay).

A song that has no chorus and one "A" section is called *through composed*. "I Remember Sky" by Stephen Sondheim is one example. "The Chair" by Dean Dillon and Hank Cochran is another. And of course, there are many form variations. For unusual song forms, check out They Might Be Giants, The B-52s, Nina Hagen, Annie Lennox, Joni Mitchell, Seal, Hootie and the Blowfish, and Prince.

LINGO REGARDING MELODY

Motif: a sequence of two to eight notes; a little kernel of melody. Some ways to vary the motif while staying close to it are:

Retrograde: reversing the motif (i.e. making it bilaterally symmetrical across the vertical axis).

Inversion: turning the motif upside down (i.e. making it bilaterally symmetrical across the horizontal axis).

Transposition: lifting or lowering the whole motif by starting on a place in the scale. For example, the first three notes of the melody of "Three Blind Mice" are repeated and transposed in the next line, "see how they run."

In the following diagram

O = the original melody

R = the retrograde melody

I = the inverted melody

R + I = both reversed and inverted melody

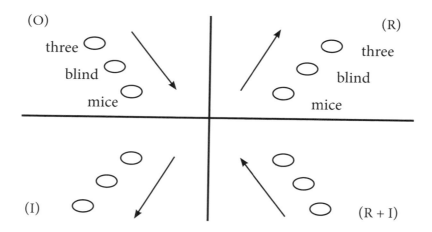

As you can see this is a wonderful way to play with and change melody. If the notes go up, try going down. Go up or down by the same amount or make intervals from the same starting point, down or up to the same starting point. "Somewhere Over the Rainbow" by Yip Harburg and Harold Arlen is an example of a melodic motif being turned around and played with throughout a piece. How about "Bottle of Wine" by Tom Paxton? Beethoven's 5th Symphony? Motifs that recur give unity and integrity to a piece of music. But they don't have to be repeated exactly to sound familiar.

Scale: stepwise motion between notes, up or down the scale.

Interval: the jumps between notes.

What our ears are used to hearing in Western music is arranged in a system of intervals that follow a pattern of whole steps between each note except notes three to four and seven to eight, which are half steps. So, counting up the scale (with uppercase roman numerals to indicate dominant tones):

1	2	3	4	5	6	7	8 or 1
do	re	mi	fa	sol	la	ti	do
I	ii	iii	IV	V	vi	vii	I
	whole step	whole step	half step	whole step	whole step	whole step	half step

The intervals are whole step, whole step, half step, whole step, whole step, whole step, half step. In the key of C, the notes are C D E F G A B C.

C, where the second C is an octave above the first.

Key: the 1, bottom, or "root" of the scale; this determines the key. Flats and sharps are used to preserve the stepwise pattern of intervals while changing keys.

Flats: going down a half step, except when the interval is already a half step between the notes. For instance, the key of C, we say C to B and F to E, we don't have the "C flat," because this is B (see *Interval*).

Sharps: going up a half step, except when the interval is already a half step between notes. We don't say E to F is "E sharp," because this is F (see *Interval*).

Natural: when a note in the key is made to fit the pattern of steps without any sharps or flats.

APPENDIX

Accidental: a note that occurs in a piece of music outside its key.

Enharmonic: on the same pitch (sound) of the note.

Chromatic: moving up and down the scale by half steps.

Diatonic: the melody moves up and down the scale with no sharps or flats. In C major, those notes would be all the white keys on a piano: C D E F G A B C.

Tessatura: the highest note in the piece, where most of the melody hangs out.

LINGO REGARDING HARMONY

Third: two notes that are two notes away from each other. The higher note is a third up. A major third is two steps away. A minor third is 1 1/2 steps away.

Triad: three notes forming a chord.

Tetrachord: four notes forming a chord.

Major triad: two whole steps and 1 1/2 steps, or a major third and a minor third. Example in the key of C: C E G, (C).

Minor triad: 1 1/2 steps and two steps, or a minor third and a major third. Example in the key of C: C E♭ G, (C min).

Dominant seventh: example in the key of C: C E G B♭ (C7).

Major seventh: example in the key of C: C E G B, (Cmaj7).

Minor seventh: example in the key of C: C E♭ G B♭, (Cmin7).

Diminished triad: flat (1/2 step down) both the non-root notes of the triad. Example in the key of C: C E♭ G♭, (Cdim).

Diminished seventh: flat (1/2 step down) all the notes in the dominant seventh but the root.

Example in the key of C: C E♭ G♭ A, (Cdim7, C°, sometimes Cdim).

Augmented triad: sharp (1/2 step up) the third note of the triad (two stacked major thirds).

Example in the key of C: C E G♯, (C⁺).

Augmented seventh: sharp (1/2 step up) the third note of the dominant seventh chord.

Example in the key of C: C E G♯ B♭, (C7⁺).

Circle of 5ths: (really the circle of 4ths) is a way of cycling through key changes, so that each position in the circle is four notes away from the next one; you are either moving up a fourth or down a fifth. The circle is a cycle of dominant or 5 (V) chords. C is the 5 chord of F, which is the 5 chord of B♭ which is the 5 chord of E♭, which is the 5 chord of A♭, and so on. The relative minor is the note 1/4 turn of the circle to the right. The relative minor has the same number of accidentals as its relative major. As you go around the circle, you add one accidental per key.

Modulation: changing key; also called *transposition*.

Enharmonic modulation: the whole scale transposed up or down but changing keys that share that note. A nifty, common way to modulate from one key to another is to progress gradually, e.g., 1 → 2 → 5 → 1 in the new key.

Mode: the whole scale transposed up or down but preserving the pattern of intervals. The arrangement of whole steps and half steps is moved to a different starting place, but the intervals between the sol and fa syllables, or notes, remains constant. The notes referred to in describing the following modes are those used in the C major scale (the white keys on a piano, no sharps or flats):

APPENDIX

Ionian: the typical major mode, the one our ears are used to hearing, starting and ending on "do" (C).

Dorian: starts and ends on "re" (D). "Eleanor Rigby" (Lennon and McCartney) is in this mode.

Phrygian: starts and ends on "mi" (E).

Lydian: starts and ends on "fa" (F).

Mixolydian: starts and ends on "sol" (G). "Take The Money and Run" (Steve Miller) "Sweet Home Alabama" (Lynyrd Skynrd) and "Norwegian Wood" (Lennon and McCartney) are in this mode.

Aeolian: the minor mode, starts and ends on "la" (A).

Locrian: starts and ends on "ti" (B).

Nashville Notation: a way of writing down chords without respect to key signature, in terms of relative internals. The tonic or root chord of a key is 1, 2 is the chord one step up from that, 3 is the third, and so on up the scale. Usually, 4/4 time is assumed unless otherwise noted, so the chords are written in groups of four.

Superscripts mean the following:
"⁻" means minor, so 6⁻ is a "six minor" chord. In the key of C, that would be Amin, Am or A⁻
"°" means diminished.
"⁺" means augmented.
"▲" means major with dominant seventh, or the 9ᵗʰ" chord.

A chord that is written with a diagonal line or a horizontal line and another number denotes the chord and its bass note. For example, "1/3" means a 1 chord with a 3 bass note. In the key of C, that would be C with an E in the bass. Split bars are also denoted with parentheses or underlining the chords.

A chord that is written with a vertical line and another number denotes a split bar. For example: In 4/4 time, "1|5" means two beats of the 1 chord and two beats of the 5 chord. Split bars are also indicated by parentheses or underlined.

A diamond shape around a number indicates a whole note over the chord.

My website and the liner notes of my CDs contain chord charts in Nashville notation, the better to teach and pitch my songs to people who might like to play them and record them. I hope this catches on and more people provide their charts to the public.

Here's a sample chord chart for a song of mine called "'Til the Cows Come Home," arranged by Jamey Whiting and Howard Schwartz. It's written to be played in the key of D, and it has two separate endings:

'Til the Cows Come Home

INTRO:	1/6-	2-/5	1/6-	2-/5
VERSE:	1	1	4	3-
	4	1/6-	2	5
CHORUS:	4	1	4	3-
	4	1/6-	2-/5	
TURNAROUND: (1)	1/6-	2-/5		
(2) 1/5				
VERSE:	1	1	4	3-
	4	1/6-	2	5
CHORUS:	4	1	4	3-
	4	1/6-	2-/5	
TAGS:	1/6-	2-/5		
	1/6	2-/5		
(FADE)				

APPENDIX

LINGO REGARDING RHYTHM

Rhythm is the pattern of beats. Tempo is how fast they are played within the units of rhythm, measures, or bars. Here are some sample rhythms or meters and their dance styles:

4/4 The most common time, sometimes written "**C**". The top number in a time signature refers to the number of beats per measure, the bottom number tells you which note value gets a count of one beat.
4 = beats per measure
4 = quarter note gets the count of one beat
Back beat: the "up" beats, e.g., One AND two AND (i.e., beats 2 and 4 of a song in 4/4).
Typically, the back beats are the ANDs.
Examples: some 4/4 dances can be found in rock and roll, as well as the rumba, the fox trot, and the cha cha.

2/2 This rhythm is divisible by twos, or duple; a gavotte (even and slow), or Peabody (fast).

2/4 Also achieved by "cutting time" of 4/4 in half to feel faster.
Examples: Morris dance, paso doble, tango, reel, hornpipe, polka, marches, swing, and fast Western swing.

3/4 This rhythm is divisible by threes, or triple. Viennese waltzes emphasizes the downbeat. Cajun waltzes emphasize all three beats. In jazz waltzes, beat 2 is pushed early:
3 = beats per measure
4 = quarter note gets the count of one beat.
Examples: waltz, mazurka, polka-waltz.

Some 8 to the bar timings are: 6/8, 12/8 (exemplified by a lot of Fats Domino's songs), and 8/8 (e.g., jig, two-step, tarantella). A slip jig is in 9/8 time. These rhythms can be accented in threes *or* twos, so they can give rise to interesting combinations.

APPENDIX

In the following notation, a dot signifies a rest, a number signifies a beat, and a letter "e" or "a" signifies a count that is off the beat.

A shuffle has triplets that leave out the middle of each group of three notes in a four-beat phrase, e.g., 1 · a 2 · a 3 · a 4 ·, dragging over the first note for two thirds the duration of the phrase and having the last note one third the duration of the phrase. If you were walking to this, a shuffle would be a limp.

A half-time shuffle, hop hop, or jack swing is in triplets:
1 e a and e a 2 e a and e a 3 e a and 4 a 4 e a and e a.
Or in shuffle time:
1 · a and · a 2 · and · a 3 · and · a 4 · and · a.

I learned this partly from Cat Cohen and partly from dancing to a lot of rap, ballroom and disco myself. As music becomes more rhythmically sophisticated, it of course, tends to borrow from other cultures. African, Cuban, and Brazilian music have several grooves layered and alternating on top of one another.

Salsa is a combination of triplets over 4/4: 123, 123 . . . and · 123, · 12, · 123, · 12.

Sixteen beats to the bar (four notes per beat) is most common in modern rock, rap, pop, R & B, and country rock writing: 1 e and a 2 e and a 3 e and a 4 e and a.

There are lots of unusual rhythms in Balkan dancing: 5/4, 3/2, 5/8, 7/8, even 9/8 is not uncommon in that tradition John Knowles wrote "Chihuahua Waltz" in 10/8 time: 123, 123, 12, 12. Glen Hanzer, in scoring the film *Once*, wrote "When Your Mind is Made Up" in 5/4 time signature, was working with a great Czech vocalist and composer Marketa Irglova at the time, which may be why that rhythm occurred to him.

Note to self: Self, get 'em DANCING! I've come to believe that what excites people to move in response to music usually involves removing one or more beats in a phrase, such as removing the 1 count in Reggae music. Our bodies move forward to supply the "missing" beat.

APPENDIX

LINGO REGARDING LYRICS

Lyrics are not literary; they are auditory. Sound über sense! Poetry is different from lyrics in that lyrics are intended to be sung. As such, the first thing to check out in a lyric is its singability. Long vowels, especially "ay," "I," "ooh," and diphthongs (two or more vowels together), at the ends of lines make for more singable lyrics. Using lots of short vowels and consonants creates a more percussive lyric with more emphasis and abruptness. This is especially appropriate in R & B or rock lyrics where the message may be urgent or aggressive.

SOME USEFUL POETIC DEVICES:

Alliteration: same beginnings of words.

Assonance: same vowel sounds of words.

Parallel structure: one part of the lyric uses the same grammatical structure as another (e.g., using a list versus subject/predicate form).

Rhyme: same sounds of words in a continuum of perfect matching to near-rhymes or assonance. How many rhymes you use affects the speed of the line delivery. Lots of inner rhymes or multiple-syllable rhymes gives a fast, light effect to a lyric. Unusual rhymes are sometimes funny: "skeleton" and "gelatin" is funnier than "heart" and "apart" and might belong in a Broadway-style piece because of its cleverness.

Scope: The scope of the language uses parallel structure, too. For example, you'd compare apples and oranges but not apples and fruit because fruit is a set that contains apples and is more general than apples. Similarly, you wouldn't have a prizefighter talk like a ten-year-old girl. Lyrics pay attention to the character and point of view of the speaker. What they talk about and how they talk about it is their "universe of discourse." Make sure you keep consistency in that department, as well as who is speaking and when, throughout the song.

Scansion, or scanning: how the accents fall on the syllables of words to achieve a rhythmic pattern.

APPENDIX

Prosody: how the words fit the music. Usually, good scansion results in good prosody.

Inflections: When putting a melody to a lyric, read it out loud first and see how the rising and falling inflections or the emphases you place on certain syllables give rise to pitches and rhythms. The natural drama of ordinary speech is musical. Use the following symbols to diagram your inflections:

/	=	accented sound
U	=	unaccented sound
/U	=	trochee
U/	=	iamb
·/ U U	=	dactyl
U U /	=	anapest
/ /	=	spondee

Metrical feet: the number of groups of syllables in a phrase. For example, iambic pentameter = 5 "feet" of iambs.

Put words or phrases together that sound like the rhythms you want to remember and repeat them:

Butternut squash	/UU/
Ricochet	/U/
One more cup of soup	UU/U/
There you go, cowboy	/U//U
It's easy for you to say	UUUU/U/
Slow down, son	/ / /
Talk with the elephant, walk with the elephant	/UU/UU,/UU/UU
Remember believing	U/UU/U
Sentimental journey	/U/U/U

Regarding My Own Songwriting Process

My writing process is more like digital filtering than synthesis. This means I often work with my mental library and tease out, or do signal conditioning, on sound, rather than building it block by block from scratch. In order words, I work like a digital filter, which starts with noise and pulls out frequencies of interest, rather than adding sine waves. I use the songs I've already heard—I have a huge mental library to draw from—and I transform and deform those sounds. Without formal training in music, I use my informal training instead. I use my "inner hearing."

Inner hearing requires a certain amount of memory for melody. You can train yourself to do this in the same fashion that you might train your spatial abilities, i.e., by holding melody in your "inner ear." (In spatial thinking, this would be analogous to imagining a picture in your "mind's eye.") Yes, these faculties do exist! See the amazing work of Stanford cognitive psychologist Roger Shepherd if you don't believe me!

Recall notes or tunes you just heard and see how many you can put together in a row. In my class at PSGW, I asked people to sing their names to each other, playing with add-ons. Most songs have a signature motif or hook to help you remember them. Once you can remember melodies, see if you can hold them in your head long enough to change them.

I use Cartesian graphs and other geometrical models of my melodies, and I generally play with melodic motifs as logical units, rather than with single notes. (See "Lingo Regarding Melody" in the appendix for some ways to play with motifs.)

REGARDING MY OWN SONGWRITING PROCESS

In film scoring, typically whole passages will be linked to a character or some action, and then those blocks of music will be reprised and treated the same way melodic motifs are treated in songs. We write overtures. Repetition, repetition, repetition. I use the smallest possible piece of melodic information, the motif, and then work with it over and over.

It's the better part of valor to stay on a note and sequence harmonies underneath, or change melodies stepwise, or use fewer notes, or use recognizable chord progressions. Who *says* you have to be sophisticated? I'm living proof that you can write songs with zero chops. Yes, Virginia, simplicity *is* a virtue.

I pay attention to bass lines to indicate arrangements, and I try to keep something stationary, either the bass line (as in Celtic music) or the melody note (as in Brazilian music). Bill Piburn taught me this. When I asked him how he wrote such wonderful melodies, he said that most people underestimate the power of staying where they are; they wander too much. See if you can stay a long tine in one place melodically or harmonically while contrasting it with some other element that you change.

Writing a capella has low cartage (it's very portable) and it doesn't obfuscate melodic ideas by fancy arrangement ideas. I can tell if I'm staying on one note or boring myself. I can take my writing into the shower or down to the beach. And best of all, my melodies are more likely to be memorable because I have to remember them, and more likely to be singable because I sing them.

What I'm really trying to say in this book is don't wait to be a genius to write your songs—no hard feelings, geniuses. Just take a deep breath and *go* for it. What have you got to lose? Your pride? Pride schmide! Your dignity? Dignity schmignity! The undying respect and admiration of your family? Now *there's* a concept! On the other hand, just suppose that they don't go in for that kind of thing. Parents are rarely overjoyed by their musical offspring. You are still who you are, with or without anybody's permission or approval.

Sure, you're brave and passionate. You have to be to engage in any art whatsoever. I'm not talking about being an iconoclast; I'm talking about having integrity and the courage of your convictions. If you didn't have something to say, you wouldn't be doing this. But keep your eye on the birdy. There are small, selfish dreams and there are big ones. We can all be dreaming and living and loving more expansively. What are you waiting for? We've got stuff to do. I dare you.

Selected Bibliography

The list below, in order of the song idea number in which they appear, are those writings and songs from which I quote an entire line or verse. This bibliography is by no means a complete record of all the works and sources I have consulted.

SONG IDEA 17
Spooner, Ken and Williams, Kim. "If The Devil Danced (In Empty Pockets)." Sony/ATV Tunes LLC and Texas Wedge Music, ©1989. All rights on behalf of Sony/ATV Tunes LLC administered by Sony/ATV Music Publishing, 8 Music Square West, Nashville, TN 37203. All Rights Reserved. Used by Permission.

SONG IDEA 105
Bonoff, Karla. "Home." Sky Harbor Music (BMI), ©1977.

SONG IDEA 122
Hughes, Elaine Farris. *Writing from the Inner Self.* New York: Harper Collins, 1991.

SONG IDEA 268
Wainwright, Loudon III. "The Swimming Song." Snowden Music (ASCAP), ©1973. Used by permission.

SONG IDEA 302
Hammerstein, Oscar II and Rodgers, Richard. "Impossible" from the musical *Cinderella* Williamson Music Co. (ASCAP), ©1964.

SELECTED BIBLIOGRAPHY

SONG IDEA 302

Hammerstein, Oscar II and Rodgers, Richard. "Do I Love You Because You're Beautiful?" Williamson Music Co. (ASCAP), ©1964.

SONG IDEA 322

King, Carole. "You've Got a Friend" Colgems EMI Music Inc. (ASCAP). Administered by Hal Leonard Corporation, ©1971.

SONG IDEA 486

Bush, Louis F. and Sherman, Allan. "Hello Mudduh, Hello Fadduh" (A Letter From Camp). Warner Chappell Music/Burning Bush Music. Used by Permission, ©1963.

INTRODUCTION TO THE SECOND 500 SONGWRITING IDEAS

James, Brett and Verges, Troy. "Who I Am" (Jessica Andrews) Album: *Who I Am*, DreamWorks, ©2001.

SONG IDEA 546

Coryat, Karl and Nick Dobson. *The Frustrated Songwriters' Handbook*. Milwaukee: Backbeat Books Hal Leonard, 2005.

SONG IDEA 610

American Way magazine "Fast Company" April 1, 2002.

SONG IDEA 615

Hong, Howard, trans. Essay "From the Pages of One Still Living," *Philosophical Fragments*. New Jersey: Princeton Paperbacks, Princeton, 1985.

SONG IDEA 630

Braheny, John. *The Craft and Business of Songwriting*. New York: Writers' Digest.

SELECTED BIBLIOGRAPHY

SONG IDEA 631

"Soup's On" recorded by Adler and Hearne *Opposites Attract*, Spring Hollow Records, ©2005.

SONG IDEA 633

Herbert, Frank. *Chapter House Dune*. New York: G. P. Putnam Sons, 1985.

SONG IDEA 633

Sturgeon, Theodore. *God Body*. New York: Donald I. Fine, 1986.
Hiatt, John. CD *Bring the Family* A&M Records, ©1987.

SONG IDEA 655

Carlyle, Thomas. Lecture 3, May 12, 1840, "The Hero as Poet" from *Carlyle's Complete Works*, Edinburgh: Sterling Edition.

SONG IDEA 657

From a lesson Fernando Sor gave to Andre Segovia, Etude in C Major.

SONG IDEA 667

Huxley, Aldus. *The Doors of Perception*. London: HarperCollins, 1977.

SONG IDEAS 689 AND 948

Talley, Gary. *Guitar Playing for Songwriters*. Video.

SONG IDEA 713

Carroll, Lewis. *Alice in Wonderland*. London: 1865, New York: Reprinted McMillan.

SONG IDEA 714

Sierra Magazine 1996.

SONG IDEA 744

Deutsch, Babbette. Poem by Rolphe Humphries from *Poetry Handbook*. New York: HarperCollins, 1982.

SELECTED BIBLIOGRAPHY

SONG IDEA 748

Milosz, Czeslaw. "A Year After Your Death" a poem from *New and Collected Poems*. New York: Ecco, 2001.

SONG IDEA 773

Roethke, Theodore. "Journey to the Interior" a poem from *The Far Field*. Garden City: Double Day, 1964.

SONG IDEA 787

Frost, Robert. An essay, "The Figure a Poem Makes." Published as a preface to his *Collected Poems*. New York: Hope, 1939.

SONG IDEA 791

Reeves, Judy. *Writing Alone, Writing Together*. New York: New World Library, 2002.

SONG IDEA 791

Wood, Jill. *Successful Songwriters Secrets* (e-book) published by www.valleyplanet.com.

SONG IDEA 796

Shaffer, Rómeldo. A quotation by her found on Jill Wood's site.

SONG IDEA 802

Lamott, Anne. *Bird by Bird*. New York: Anchorage Doublday, 1997.

SONG IDEA 820

Catlett, Joyce and Robert Firestone. *Psychological Defenses in Everyday Life*. New York: Human Sciences Press, 1989.
Maisel, Eric. *Coaching the Artist Within*. Novato, CA: New World Library, 2005.

SONG IDEA 821

The Song of the Lark. Boston: Houghton Mifflin, 1915. Dickenson, Emily. The quotation is a comment made to Thomas Higgenson, 1890 posthumously published poetry.

SELECTED BIBLIOGRAPHY

SONG IDEA 837

Ueland, Brenda. *If you Want to Write*. New York: G. P. Putnam & Son, 1939.

SONG IDEA 845

Blake, William. "Jerusalem," Princeton: Princeton University Press, self-published and collected in reprint, 1991.

SONG IDEA 848

Phillips, Elizabeth. *Marianne Moore*. New York: Unger Publishing Company, 1982.

SONG IDEA 855

Busch, Fredrich. *Dangerous Profession: A Book About The Writing Life*. New York: St. Martins Press, 1998.

SONG IDEA 887

Adams, James Lowell. *Conceptual Blockbusting*. Cambridge: Perseus Publishing, 1974.
De Bono, Edward. *The Use of Lateral Thinking*. London: Pelican Press, 1967.
Feynman, Richard: *Surely You're Joking, Mr. Feynman!* New York: W. W Norton Company, 1985.
Feynman, Richard. *What Do You Care What Other People Think?* New York: W. W. Norton Company, 1988.

SONG IDEA 934

Danko, Harold. Article in *Down Beat* magazine, May 16, 2003

SONG IDEA 1000

"What Are You Waiting For?" from the album *The Three-Legged Dog and Other Tales*, In Cahoots Music, ©2004

Also, I'd like to recommend a book that I agree with wholeheartedly: *The Anatomy of Melody by Alice Parker*, GIA Publications ©2006, and a DVD from Deering Banjos: *Composing on Claw Hammer Banjo by Jens Kruger.*

Index

Songs (unless otherwise indicated) listed by idea number

INDEX

INDEX

INDEX

INDEX

INDEX

INDEX

INDEX

INDEX

INDEX

Songwriters, Lyricists, Composers listed by idea number

INDEX

INDEX

INDEX

INDEX

INDEX

INDEX

INDEX

INDEX

About the Author

Lisa Aschmann is a prolific and professional songwriter, a singer, and an educator. She has recorded six CDs of her own and has had hundreds of songs recorded (with hundreds more yet to be recorded!) by major artists in almost every genre from bluegrass to jazz, country, folk, inspirational, pop, and R & B. She lives in Nashville, Tennessee. Her web site is www.songwritingideas.com. Her email address is: nashvlgeo@aol.com, named after her music publishing company, Nashville Geographic (ASCAP).

Her latest releases are: "Boom Boom Boom" with Joel Evans in the film, *Bonneville* and "Until It Happens to You" in the television show, *Shark*; "Tall in the Saddle" with John Tirro in the film, *Horses and Men;* and "The Spiral Arms" with Tom Kimmel recorded by Joe Chemay and Celeste Krenz.

MORE ABOUT THE AUTHOR

If we in this country had the sense they have in Japan, Lisa Aschmann would be counted as one of our National Living Treasures in songwriting. There is a reason so many of the great songwriters in Nashville have sought her out as co-writer, know and marvel at her work; and that young writers show up like pilgrims at her door, a songwriter's Nadia Boulanger. There is a reason that Lisa remains my favorite co-writer after more than 15 years of writing together, that I feel as if I've stolen one more day of heaven from fate every day I get to sit and write with her.

The reason? Lisa is far more than a great songwriter, though Lord knows she is that. Mistress of melody, with an encyclopedic knowledge of songs from every genre and era that she uses to sculpt timeless tunes out of thin air. Consummate lyricist who remembers that songwriter's deeper mission—to re-exalt the language of their day, remind us of where we came from and where we are going. Fearless writer who can "dare to be stupid" as she likes to say—be silly, whimsical, profound, prophetic, humble, ironic by turns; who can let ideas flow with complete freedom, then labor absorbed and patient for hours making sure every word, every note is exactly the best and truest it could be. Such a rare marriage of spontaneity and craft, the big picture and sweating the small details, is part of what makes Lisa one of the great songwriters of our time.

But beyond all that is the sheer radiant joy in creativity that is her calling, her creed that brooks no denomination, her essence. Time spent in Lisa's presence is like offering up incense in the very Temple of the Creative Spirit. Just walk into her house—crowded not only with CDs, drawers crammed with demos of the thousands of songs she's written, books on music—but as well with groaning bookshelves over-flowing with books on every conceivable subject—theoretical astronomy to Greek rhetoric, to the lives of saints and the songs of birds—all gathered according to an inscrutable order that only she can fathom, by which everything is connected to everything. It is a songwriter's paradise. I've never plucked a series of guitar chords in her earshot without that famous pen of hers immediately starting to move over the paper—as stories and characters arise out of nowhere.

Most people ask: How can we be creative? Where do ideas for songs come from? In Lisa's world, the question is: When did we ever start believing so little in ourselves as to doubt creativity for a moment? What beautiful odd detail of this world is not worthy of a song?

Lisa is unceasingly curious about every unsung mystery in our universe (and ready to sing about it). She is unfailingly hopeful in the midst of this difficult world and her own life, in which she has braved difficulties that would have turned most of us bitter and cynical. Lisa can break your heart with a song about a potato, can read the notes left on God's refrigerator, just happens to have read all of St. Augustine's Confessions and knows why he stole the pear. And she, like God, has forgiven him.

—Mark Simos, Songwriter and Professor, Songwriting,
Berklee College of Music